THE

AND SILVER

BUYER'S HANDBOOK

Raffi Katz

THIS EDITION PUBLISHED IN 2010 BY

QUICKTEST
PO BOX 180
WATFORD
WD1 5JD

British Library Cataloguing Data

Katz, Raffi
      The gold and silver buyer's handbook
      4th ed.
      1. Gold trades   2. Silver trades
      1. Title
      380.1'4241

      ISBN 978-0-9512095-3-0

Printed in Great Britain by
Tiger Press, tigerpress.alan@googlemail.com

*The front cover shows someone testing gold using a glass bottle of acid and a spatula
applicator. Many acid bottles are plastic, with a dropper instead of a spatula.*

CONTENTS

PART ONE: GOLD AND SILVER

PART TWO: BUYING AND SELLING

SELLING:

BUYING:

BUYING AND SELLING FOR PROFIT:

PART THREE: USEFUL INFORMATION AND FASCINATING FACTS

ACKNOWLEDGEMENTS

Acknowledgement is given to THE BRITISH HALLMARKING COUNCIL and the HALLMARKING CONVENTION for their permission to print illustrations of hallmarks.

I would like to thank the following people. Bernard Priceman for teaching me scrap-buying and bullion-dealing; Gail Hislop PJ Gem Dip, PJ Val Dip, FNAG, MIRV for helping with the section on valuations; Michael Bloomstein for updating me with regulations concerning bullion; Phil Davis for taking the cover photograph; Sara for proof-reading; and the great many people in the jewellery trade and at the antiques fairs who were so eager to offer advice.

TERMINOLOGY

Jewellers often use the term 'metal' to mean 'not gold or silver'. So you might say to a jeweller, "Is it gold or is it metal?". In this book I use the term in its chemical sense: gold and silver are metals.

The purity of gold (the amount of actual gold in the alloy) can be measured in parts per thousand or in carat. Other words for purity are *standard, fineness*, carat, Karat, karatage.

I often refer to *secondhand* items. This includes 'pre-owned' items such as unwanted presents. They are secondhand, even if they are un-used.

Part of this book is guidance for 'private individuals' and part is very specifically for traders. If you deal in gold and silver as hobby, are you a trader? You are a trader if you sell goods that are not your personal property, attend sales regularly, employ someone to help with the sale, and/or sell goods at a number of venues generating a regular income.

I sometimes refer to *Britain* and sometimes to the *United Kingdom (UK)* and sometimes to the British Isles. Britain (sometimes called *Great Britain, GB)* is England Scotland and Wales. The UK includes Northern Ireland. The British Isles includes all islands including Southern Ireland.

INTRODUCTION

This is a unique book of information for all those who buy or sell gold or silver, jewellery or coins. It also contains a large amount of information of use to the general antiques trader.

The book started, unknowingly, when I worked at a shop specialising in coins, medals, jewellery and bullion. From the very first day I started making lists and charts: formulae of how to calculate bullion prices quickly, lists of coins which were of value, notes about how I had mistaken non-gold items for gold...the information grew and grew. The reason for this enthusiasm was simple. We advertised widely; we dealt within the trade, both locally and abroad; we saw customers who called into the shop and it was very busy, there was no time to spend minutes researching each enquiry, the answers had to be to hand.

In the shop I soon learnt that the skill in determining values was in knowing what was worthless and what was worth researching. Every day callers from around the country would telephone: had their set of medallions appreciated in value? are some gold sovereigns worth more than bullion value? how much is gold worth? To my amazement I found myself answering the same questions day after day. The answers are in this book.

Some of the information was hard to come by. Sets of commemorative medallions are beautiful but most end up in the melting pot. How much are they worth? They are worth the weight of gold or silver. How much do they weigh? Nobody knew, even the manufacturers could not tell us. So each time we broke the seals on a set of medallions we weighed them - the list of weights is in this book. This book includes many other charts of weights and values as well as clear explanations of carat and hallmarks.

Upon leaving the shop I went into business on my own, manufacturing and marketing testing equipment for gold, silver and gemstones along with magnifiers and weighing scales. We manufacture the QUICKTEST and TROYTEST precious metal testers.

With the growth of the internet (which didn't existed when I wrote the first edition of this book) came our website, www.quicktest.co.uk, and over the last few years I have written several articles in answer to customers' questions. How do you clean silver using a simple chemical reaction rather than resorting to messy cleaners? If your weighing machine no longer gives accurate readings, how do you recalibrate it? What are the latest laws on using weighing machines for use in trade? How do you transfer money from one bank to another, for free, and know that it will arrive in two hours? What do you need to know about handling testing acids? Which are the latest electronic gold testers and how reliable are they? Now that there are so many companies offering to buy gold, where will you get the best rate? What are the pitfalls in taking credit cards? The answers are in this book.

Raffi Katz
May 2010
raffi@quicktest.co.uk

PART ONE
GOLD AND SILVER

PURITY

Pure gold (otherwise known as fine gold) is rarely[1] used for making items, it is too soft. Coins would wear away,[2] rings and bangles would bend out of shape. Before manufacture other metals[3] are added to the melting pot of gold. The result is an alloy, part gold and part other metal. Colloquially we still term the metal 'gold' even though it is no longer pure. We do, however, qualify the word 'gold' by stating the purity - the 'standard' to which the gold has been refined, also referred to as 'the standard of fineness' or simply 'the standard' – all these terms mean 'purity'.

Purity is measured in two scales. Parts per thousand and carat. 'Parts per Thousand' is percentage (parts per hundred) with the decimal point moved one place to the right[4]. You may, for instance, put into the melting pot 750 parts per thousand (75.0%) pure gold and 25 parts per thousand (25.0%) other metals. 1000 parts per 1000 is pure gold, though the chemists have decided that gold *that* pure is difficult to make and so 'pure' gold bars are marked 999, i.e. 999 parts per thousand (99.9%).

The carat scale uses the figure 24 as a definition of pure gold: 24 parts per 24 = pure gold; instead of measuring in thousandths it measures in 24ths. So 12 parts per 24 (12ct) would be 50% (500 parts per thousand).

Many different purities are used around the world, in the UK we have traditionally used five: 9ct (·375); 14ct (·585); 15ct (·625); 18ct (·750) and 22ct (·916). EU rulings have now forced the UK to add 950 and 999 parts per thousand, though these are not marked in carat since they don't convert to exact numbers (22.8ct and 23.98ct respectively).

Silver purity is measured in parts per thousand only. In the UK we use 800 ('continental' silver), 925 (Sterling Silver), 958 (Britannia Silver) and 999 ('pure' silver).

---

[1] A few coins are made of a purity better than 22ct. These are bullion coins rather than circulation coins. The only jewellery I have seen which is better than 22ct comes from China and the Far East; Indian gold is usually 22ct and Arab gold 20ct or 21ct.

[2] The first durable gold alloy of 990 purity (ie. 99 per cent pure, 23¾ct) was developed in 1990 - the remaining 1% is titanium.

[3] Silver, copper and zinc are added to the mixture. These metals also alter the colour: silver gives a yellow/greenish tint, copper red and zinc white; and the correct proportions of silver and copper produce the same bright yellow of the original fine gold.

[4] Although people tend to refer to this as 'decimal' it is actually the Mili Decimal system.

This chart shows common standards used in other countries.

Gold Standards in the European Union in parts per thousand										
	Legal minimum in carats	333	375	500	585	750	833	875	916	990	999
Austria	9		x		x	x					
Belgium					x	x	x				
Denmark	8	x			x	x					
Finland					x	x					
France	9		x		x	x					
Germany		x			x	x			x		
Greece	8	x	x		x	x			x		x
Ireland	9		x		x	x			x		
Italy		x	x	x	x	x	x				
Luxembourg					x	x	x				
Netherlands					x	x	x		x		
Portugal	9				x	800					
Spain					x	x					
Sweden					x	840			975		
United Kingdom	9		x		x	x			x	x	x

Chart from Goldavenue Encyclopaedia (see info.goldavenue.com/) and Gold Fields Mineral Services Ltd (see www.gfms.co.uk).

TYPES OF GOLD

Pure gold is pure gold. Like petrol which has been refined to an agreed standard or distilled water which has been distilled to an agreed standard, the result is homogenous. A litre of petrol in Cardiff is the same as a litre of petrol in Aberdeen and, likewise, an ounce of pure gold is the same everywhere. The only variation is in the *standard* to which the petrol or gold has been refined.

So, apart from the purity (and the 'additives' can alter the colour, see PURITY above) are there any 'types' of gold?

The short answer is no. For instance, how does Welsh gold differ from South African gold? Answer: it doesn't. There is absolutely no way of telling one from the other. So why is Welsh gold 'worth' so much more than other gold? Answer: the *gold value* is exactly the same as any other gold. but the product (jewellery) being sold is not really just 'gold' but also a romantic image of Wales.

There is an interesting story concerning Welsh gold that illustrates the difference between the value of gold as a raw metal and the value of gold jewellery. The Clogau St David's gold mine produced just 40 ounces of gold between 1980 and 1989 by which time the one gold-producing vein was all but exhausted. The owners planned to re-open the mine as a tourist attraction but the plans had to be abandoned when they were refused permission to build a cable car up the mountain. It eventually closed down in 1995. Meanwhile, the mine-owners can quite truthfully say that the little remaining gold they have is, perhaps, the rarest in the world and that each item of jewellery contains[1] some of it. It is this romantic image that adds to the value of 'Welsh gold' jewellery. Similarly, at the Parys Mountain mine most of the income was from zinc, copper, lead and silver, yet the increased 'value' of Welsh gold merited the added cost of gold extraction at the rate of 0.5 grams per tonne (usually extraction is uneconomical if the yield is less than 10 grams per tonne[2]). In all cases the intrinsic value of the gold does not change with 'rarity'.

Rose gold is a rich red colour of gold produced, typically, in Victorian times. In the first edition of this book I echoed the oft-heard rumour that 'they can't match the old red-tinted gold of Victorian times'. This was true, jewellers couldn't...because nobody would buy it. Today 'rose' red gold is back in fashion and so jewellery manufacturers have found that they *can* make it.

There are many other techniques for combining precious metals, though they are not generally seen in this country[3] because they cannot be hallmarked (you cannot have a selection of hallmarks on one item). Some examples are: layering and rolling[4] layers of platinum and different coloured gold, a bit like rolling different colours of Plasticine in your hand; filigree (fine wires) made of a mixture of platinum and 18ct strands; inlaying a wire of one colour onto a background of another (eg. an initial or logo on cufflinks); rolling layers of different metals then removing parts of the top layer (by engraving or etching with acid) to reveal the colour below.

---

[1] 'Containing' Welsh gold does not mean that the items are made entirely of Welsh gold, but that into the melting pot of gold went mostly silver, copper and zinc, then 'non-Welsh' gold, and, finally, a 'measured amount' of Welsh gold.

[2] One metric tonne equals 1000Kg.

[3] Though some antique rings are made with platinum settings soldered onto an 18ct yellow gold shank (it was fashionable to have rings in yellow gold, but diamonds display best against white)

[4] Strips of the precious metal are put through steel mangles

NOT GOLD

Often I would test an item, the customer would wait with baited breath as the acid reacted, and I would pronounce the verdict:

"It's not gold"

"What is it then?" the customer would ask.

"It's not silver or platinum either", I would reply, as if that was all the customer needed to know.

"But what *is* it?" the customer would plead.

"Metal."

"Metal?"

At this point some customers looked mildly confused. Those with a background in chemistry would try hard not to smile.

"Yes, metal. Base metal" I would conclude.

This idea, still common amongst jewellers, dates back to the alchemy of the Middle ages. There were only two types of metal, precious (*noble* metals) or worthless (*base* metals) - who needed to know more?

If your jewellery contains no gold, silver or platinum, it is certainly made of something else, probably copper or a copper-based alloy[1].

Copper is a dull yellow metal which tones to dark brown with age. If you add other metals to the copper you get the following alloys. Brass (copper and zinc), bronze (copper, zinc and tin), nickel-brass (copper, zinc, tin and nickel), or gun metal (copper, zinc, tin and lead). In all cases most of the alloy is copper.

Pinchbeck (pronounced 'pinchback') is known for its deep reddish-yellow colour and was very popular for making jewellery in the late eighteenth and early nineteenth century. The metal is named after Christopher Pinchbeck who was a London clockmaker and toy maker. He used approximately five parts copper to one part zinc. Eighteenth and nineteenth century toys, snuff boxes and jewellery are always collectable

---

[1] An alloy is a mixture of metals

if in nice condition, whatever they are made of, but items made of pinchbeck are all the more saleable for the rumour that only Mr Pinchbeck knew the exact formula which has now been lost for all time.[1] Ironically, there was no such romantic image in the late nineteenth century by which time 'Pinchbeck' had become known as an imitation of gold, cheap and deceptive.

'Back & Front' (eg. '9ct B&F') is found mostly on lockets. It means that the back and the front of the locket are solid 9ct gold but the remainder (the rims, catches, frames, loop and jump ring) are not gold.

Rolled gold comprises a sandwich made of two very thin slices of gold with a sheet of brass or steel in the middle. Similarly, Gold Filled means that the outside shell is gold and the 'filling' is not. Watch bracelets are often marked 'RG' for *Rolled Gold*. Although the layer of gold is very thin, it is thicker than the heaviest plating and must be filed quite firmly before testing with acid (see page 27) but if you see it is marked RG you will *know* it is not solid gold.

Items can be plated with gold. 'Flash' electroplating is deposited using a tank or beaker containing a gold solution.[2]   The method is known as 'flash' plating because it's very thin quick layer, like a 'flash" – but it does tend to rub off 'in a flash' too, especially when worn as jewellery and rubs against clothing or skin.[3]

Another plating process ('hard' plating) uses a vacuum process which is more durable, often guaranteed to last a few years, and advertised as such, eg. you will see on the inside of a watch back, "Guaranteed 5 Years" which means the gold plating should not wear off for that amount of time.

For details of how to test these, see the section on *Testing* on page 40.

---

[1] This cannot be true if pinchbeck was still being used in the eighteenth and nineteenth centuries because Christopher Pinchbeck died in 1732. Comments from historians welcome.

[2] Using a DC power supply (it can be an ordinary battery) connect the positive side to a strip of copper and dangle it in the solution, then clip the negative to the actual item and dangle it in the solution. When the current flows, the item is plated.

[3] At worst it will last a few days or weeks. I have seen plating 'kits' and the suppliers say it should last several months, but it very much depends on exactly what you are plating and how thickly t is applied.

HALLMARKING

A hallmark[1] comprises three compulsory marks, the standard (fineness) mark, the office (place) mark and the sponsor's (maker's) mark. These are stamped (or laser-engraved) into the metal by an assay office.

The first compulsory mark is the *standard* mark. This shows the purity (fineness). To establish the purity a scraping[2] is taken and analysed. However, the *exact* fineness isn't marked, only one of a handful of 'standard' finenesses. For gold these are (in parts per thousand and carat): 375 (9ct), 585 (14ct), 750 (18ct), 916 (22ct); and also 990 and 999 (marked in parts per thousand only). For silver these are (in parts per thousand) 800, 925, 958 and 999.

The process of analysing a metal is called an 'assay'. The only organisation permitted to mark precious metals with hallmark stamps is The Assay Office. It is illegal for anyone else to mark precious metals, even possessing a punch that reads *9ct* is illegal.

The next part of a compulsory hallmark is the Assay Office mark which shows where the item was assayed.[3]

The third compulsory mark is the sponsor's (maker's) mark, usually their initials. Manufacturers must have their mark registered with an Assay Office. For a member of the public the Assay Office will use their own sponsor's mark, eg. BAO for *Birmingham Assay Office*.

Date letters (recorded since 1544) have not been marked on very small items since 1984 and have not been compulsory at all since 1999.

Any assay office will verify a hallmark (tell you if it's genuine) free of charge. Full assaying and hallmarking are not expensive. Bulk prices vary from 30p to £2.00 each for new items, about £6.00 each for secondhand items. You don't have to get items hallmarked in bulk, they will happily accept one item, but postage and handling will increase the cost to £10.00. All this is for a basic service that takes a few days, there are many other options, you can even have an item hallmarked in an hour if you're prepared to spend over £50.00.

---

[1] A Hallmark is so named because it was marked in the hall of the goldsmiths, Goldsmith Hall

[2] This is where we get the expression, 'To come up to scratch'

[3] There are five remaining Assay Offices in the British Isles: London, Birmingham, Sheffield, Edinburgh and Dublin, see page 177 for contact details. Five others have closed down. Norwich closed in 1701, York in 1856, Newcastle in 1883, Chester in 1962, Glasgow in 1963.

Anyone can send items to be hallmarked but a trader (anyone who sends items regularly) must have their name registered and a Sponsor's Mark stamp made. The cost of registration is under £100.00 and lasts ten years. Send items only by registered post and pack them in simple envelopes - if you use layers of paper and sticky tape the Assay Office will charge double! The Assay Office can also assay any item and tell you the exact purity without hallmarking, you should ask for a 'report only'.

Gold items are hallmarked 375, 585, 750, 916, 950 and 999 only: any item which *just* fails a test will be marked down a grade. An item submitted as 585 (14ct) which is less (eg. only 13.9 ct) will be marked 375 (9ct). If you have some Arab 21ct gold you might assume that it will be more saleable with a UK hallmark, but beware, if, at the Assay Office, it fails the 22ct test it will be hallmarked 18ct, now 'proof' to any layman that it is 18ct. A hallmark, therefore, guarantees that the item is *at least* the purity stated, not that it is *exactly* the purity stated[1].

Items made since 1973 must, by law, be hallmarked. Exceptions are made for very lightweight[2] items. The law states that items which are not hallmarked must not be described as gold, a problem for traders trying to sell antique items which are not hallmarked. Even the description of an item as 'stamped 18K' led to prosecution because the jeweller *implied* that the item was gold (which, of course, it was). If a trader tests an item in front of you and proves it is gold, then the facts of chemistry are indisputable, but do not expect a written receipt stating that it is gold.

A useful pocket book is the *Dealer Guide, English Silver Hallmarks* which enables the dating of British hallmarked items from 1544. The same date letters apply to both gold and silver. There is a also book of international silver marks published by Tardy (*International Hallmarks on Silver, collected by Tardy*) which includes an ingenious index showing marks in picture-order, since you will not be able to look up a mark under *Country* if you don't know which country the mark comes from.

The official hallmark chart must, by law, be displayed by everyone who trades in precious metals (gold, silver, platinum or Palladium), and this applies to *anyone* who buys or sells precious metals, whether in a shop, market, antiques fair or even a boot sale.

---

[1] In practice it will be *very* close because manufacturers don't want to give you more gold than you have actually paid for.

[2] Exemptions for items under the following weights: silver 7.78g, gold 1g, platinum 0.5g.

HALLMARK CHART

This is the chart that must be displayed wherever precious metals are bought or sold. It is available from the Assay Office www.theassayoffice.co.uk/tbhc.html or telephone 0871 871 6020.

Ask if it's hallmarked
IT'S YOUR GUARANTEE

In the UK it is illegal to sell or describe any item as Gold, Silver, Platinum or Palladium unless it is hallmarked*

A UK hallmark is struck by an independent assay office and guarantees the precious metal content of the item you are buying. Sellers in contravention of the law may be prosecuted and could face fines or imprisonment.

COMPULSORY MARKS

THE HALLMARK COMPRISES THREE COMPULSORY MARKS:
A SPONSOR'S MARK, A FINENESS MARK AND AN ASSAY OFFICE MARK.

Sponsor's Mark	Fineness Mark				Assay Office Mark
The registered mark of the company that submitted the article for hallmarking.	Tells you the precious metal content, expressed in parts per thousand.				Tells you which Assay Office tested and hallmarked the article.
	Silver	Palladium	Gold	Platinum	
A B	800	2009 500	375 (9 carat)	850	London
	925 (Sterling)	950	585 (14 carat)	900	Birmingham
	958 (Britannia)	999	750 (18 carat)	950	Sheffield
	999	2010 500	916 (22 carat)	999	Edinburgh
		950	990		
		999	999		

OPTIONAL MARKS — YOU MAY SEE OPTIONAL MARKS, SUCH AS THE TRADITIONAL FINENESS SYMBOL AND THE DATE LETTER DEPICTING THE YEAR THE ITEM WAS HALLMARKED.

Traditional Fineness Symbols	Sterling Silver	Sterling Silver Scotland	Britannia Silver	Palladium	Gold	Platinum
Date Letter	j 2008	k 2009	l 2010	m 2011	n 2012	o 2013
International Convention Marks	925 Silver	950 Palladium	375 Gold	950 Platinum	This mark is used by countries, including the United Kingdom, that are signatories to the International Convention on Hallmarking and is recognised by all those countries.	
Exemption Weights* Articles above these weights must be hallmarked	7.78 grams	1.0 gram	1.0 gram	0.5 grams		

What should I do if my item is not hallmarked? If you have a concern regarding hallmarking contact your local Trading Standards Authority. For more information visit www.britishhallmarkingcouncil.co.uk

Produced in Accordance with the Hallmarking Act 1973
Version 1/2010
© British Hallmarking Council

A HISTORY OF HALLMARKING

1200s to 1970s

In Britain, Goldsmith's Guilds existed in the twelfth century but it was not until 1238 that they became 'official' by order of King Henry III, who was determined to combat the selling of sub-standard[1] gold. By 1300 it was practice for the Guild of London Goldsmiths to mark approved gold items with the stamp of a leopard's head (or, rather, a lion's head[2]). Similar guilds were formed in 1423 in York, Newcastle-upon-Tyne, Lincoln, Norwich, Bristol, Salisbury and Coventry; in Scotland in 1457 and in Ireland in 1637.

The consumer laws of the fifteenth century were quite remarkable. Gilding base metal jewellery and everyday items (eg. copper covered with gold) was forbidden, the standard of gold was set at 18ct, inspectors toured the country and there was a system of fines and compensation where fraud was proved.

Successive laws in the sixteenth and seventeenth centuries strengthened the powers of the inspectors and increased the penalties. Goldsmiths were forced to register their mark and were made responsible for ensuring their items were of the standard purity, though it was not the goldsmiths but the wardens who assayed and hallmarked the gold. When it was found that corrupt wardens were marking sub-standard goods '18ct' there was an outcry from the goldsmiths who were legally responsible. The result was that each Assay Office was forced to add a date stamp. The authorities knew which officials were in charge of each Assay Office each year, and that official would be held responsible for any fraudulent hallmarking. Further laws in the eighteenth century imposed a duty payable on gold and silver as proof of payment was by way of yet another stamp, that of the monarch's head (discontinued in 1890).

With each set of laws the standard purity of gold was altered. In 1300 this standard was 19ct, from 1477 it was18ct, from 1576 it was 22ct - all marked with the emblem of a leopard. In 1798 18ct was introduced in

---

[1] 'Standard' means the standard purity accepted (legally) as 'gold', pure gold not being used because it is too soft.

[2] This mark is referred to as a leopard's head even though it is quite obviously a lion's head. The error dates back to the days when Acts of Parliament were written in old French, 'Leopard' being mistranslated as 'leopard' instead of 'lion'. The style of the lion emblem has changed over the years. In this book I follow the convention of calling it a leopard.

addition to 22ct, the 18ct standard being marked by '18ct' plus a crown instead of a leopard's head; then, in 1844, the leopard on 22ct was abolished and replaced with '22ct' and a crown. There was now (1844) no leopard on gold items. The leopard emblem continued as the standard mark on silver.

In the nineteenth century it was reaslised that the high British standards made exports to North America very expensive: North America's standard was 10ct, the British 18ct and 22ct were too expensive for the Americans. In 1854 Britain introduced three lower standards in addition to 18ct and 22ct: 15ct, 12ct and 9ct. The three lower standards were marked both in carat and parts per thousand 15ct (·625); 12ct (·500); 9ct (·375).

12ct and 15ct (typically Victorian) fell into disuse. The last change of standard was in 1932 when both 12ct and 15ct were discontinued and *today* 14ct (the standard for jewellery in Europe) was introduced. This leaves the following standards of gold in use today: 9ct (375) 14ct (585), 18ct (750) and 22ct (916).

All the standards I have listed so far were for 'wares' (manufactured articles that can be sold). The standards for coins were not always the same. Between 1300 and 1625 the standard for gold coins changed seven times, varying from 23ct to 24ct (with one brief period of 20ct, 1545 to 1549). 22ct has been used for British gold coins since 1626.

The standard for silver wares was 925 parts per thousand up to 1696. The Civil War, earlier that century, had resulted in the Royalists destroying vast numbers of silver wares. The result was a shortage of silver which led to silversmiths melting silver coins to use in manufacture. This, in turn, led to a severe shortage of silver coin. The Government responded by raising the standard of silver used for making items from 925 parts per thousand (Sterling Silver) to a new standard of 958 parts per thousand (Britannia Silver). Silversmiths could no longer melt the Sterling standard coinage for use in manufacture. When the coin supply eased, the standard was returned to Sterling, though the Britannia standard was not abolished and can still be used today.

1973 to 2010

In 1973 it was decided that the existing hallmarking laws were too complicated. The date letters, for instance, were different for each Assay Office and were changed in the middle of each year. Jewellers were still using old stamps to stamp gold '9ct', '18ct' etc. which passed as 'hallmarks' with the unwary public - the new law changed all this. At the same time, a new 'department' was set up (funded by the Assay Offices) to publicise hallmarking and advise the Government: *The British Hallmarking Council*.

All assay offices were to use the same date letter, starting with the letter 'a' in January 1975 so that the letter 'a' would recur in the year 2000. This acknowledged the fact that the main use of date letters was by collectors (up to the late nineteenth century nobody took any notice of date letters, hence one finds a mixture of dates within sets of old cutlery). Jewellers would no longer be allowed to use their own purity stamps, only the Assay Office was permitted to mark gold, and no gold could be described as 'gold' unless it was hallmarked.

For a chart of the date letters and illustrations of the Assay Office marks, see page 147.

All seemed to be sorted, until the 1990s when the buzz-word in the European Union (EU) was 'Harmonisation', heralding a Brave New World where the commonly used purities of precious metals (and their marks) would be standardised throughout Europe[1].

The UK Government (and some other countries) were in favour of 'third-party verification' - that meant independent testing and marking (like our system of Assay Offices), but others were more in favour 'self-certification' - which meant the manufacturer would test and mark the items. It was even proposed that both systems be used together.

In addition to the UK Government and the European Union, there was a third party in this 'love triangle' - the Assay Offices (along with British Hallmarking Council). They were part of a system that had been established several years earlier: The International Hallmarking Convention[2] which was independent of the EU Under this convention, items can be marked with a mark common to all the countries, a mark imaginatively called The Common Control Mark (CCM). The CCM has the same legal status as a UK hallmark, items with the CCM mark need

---

[1] The plan was to agree a *European Directive on Precious Metals*.

[2] To give it its original name, this was the *Convention on the Control of Articles of Precious Metals*, signed in Vienna in 1971 - but the name was so long that it became abbreviated to *The Vienna Convention* - another bad name, since it gives no clues as to what it might be. So, colloquially, it became known as the *International Hallmarking Convention* or just *The Hallmarking Convention*. It was eventually signed in 1972, came into force in 1975, and was ratified by Britain in 1976.

not be re-tested and re-hallmarked when imported into the UK

RESPONSIBILITY MARK	COMMON CONTROL MARK				FINENESS (PURITY) MARK			
	Platinum	Gold	Palladium	Silver	Platinum	Gold	Palladium	Silver
A B	850	375	500	800	850	375	500	800
	900	585	950	830	900	585	950	830
	950	750	999	925	950	750	999	925
	999	916		999	999	916		999
		999				999		

ASSAY OFFICE MARK

Austria Cyprus Czech Republic Denmark Finland Hungary Ireland Israel

Latvia Lithuania Netherlands Norway Poland Portugal

Slovenia Slovak Republic Sweden Switzerland United Kingdom

© Hallmarking Convention

So what happened to European 'harmonisation' on precious metals?

Answer: nothing.

After years of negotiations it simply fizzled out.[1] That left us with the original (non-EU) International Hallmarking Convention, much to the delight of the Assay Offices and the British Hallmarking Council.

---

[1] In legal terms, several years of negotiations don't just 'fizzle out'. It would be more correct to say that the draft Directive on the Control of Articles of Precious Metals was withdrawn by the European Commission due to lack of agreement.

Simple. Sorted at last, you may think. Not so! In 1994 there was a dramatic development.

A Dutch jeweller imported gold and sold it as 'gold' even though it didn't have a hallmark (it had no marks at all) and claimed, in court,[1] that this was legal under European law. The court ruled against her, the gold did need to be marked. But which marks? Answer: the marks of any EU country that used 'equivalent' systems of testing gold, and whose marks were 'intelligible' to consumers. The court also ruled that the date letter couldn't really be considered part of a hallmark.[2]

The consequence was that UK hallmark law had to be tweaked (and this is how the law stands today):

- date letters are no longer obligatory as part of a hallmark
- all seven standards (purities) of gold used throughout the EU are recognised as 'gold' (though not all hallmarked as such in the UK)
- all items are marked in Parts per Thousand (so the lion alone is no longer used to signify 'silver)
- the lower standards of .800 silver and .850 platinum are recognised as 'silver' and 'platinum'.

Overleaf is a chart I have compiled by combining three charts[3] to show countries that do and do not have hallmarking systems, some compulsory, some voluntary; some of the countries are in Europe (some belong to the European Union and some belong to the European Free Trade Association); some have hallmarking systems left over from British-colonial or French-colonial times. Those printed in bold belong to the International Hallmarking Convention (see above).[4]

---

[1] The case was Ludomira Neeltje v Barbara Houtwipper (known as The Houtwipper Case) at the European Court of Justice, 1994. British law was changed to reflect this ruling in 1998, effective as of January 1st 1999.

[2] Date letters had not been marked on small items since 1986 *for practical reasons* (i.e. if the item was so small that there wasn't space). Now, the court ruled, "...consumers have, as a rule, no interest in knowing the date of manufacture [and] the indication of the year of hallmarking may not always provide reliable information regarding the year of manufacture, since it may differ from the year in which the hallmark is affixed, above all in the case of imported goods"

[3] One is from the Assay Offices of Great Britain, two are from Goldavenue Encyclopaedia, see info.goldavenue.com/ and www.gfms.co.uk

[4] Compiling a chart of different systems used throughout the world is an almost impossible task, anyone with ideas or up-to-date data is welcome to contact me at raffi@quicktest.co.uk

Compulsory hallmarking system	Voluntary hallmarking system	No hallmarking system at all
Algeria	Belgium	Germany
Bahrain	**Denmark**	Greece
Egypt	**Finland**	Italy
Kuwait	**Sweden**	Luxembourg
Tunisia	Israel	Iceland
Austria	Lebanon	.
France	Morocco	
Ireland	Qatar	
Belorussia	Japan	
Bulgaria	Singapore	
Croatia	**Norway**	
Cyprus	**Switzerland** (jewellery)	
Czech Republic	Liechtenstein (jewellery)	
Denmark		
Estonia		
Hungary		
Ireland		
Latvia		
Lithuania		
Moldavia		
Poland		
Romania		
Russian Federation		
Slovakia		
Ukraine		
Netherlands		
Norway		
Poland		
Portugal		
Spain		
Slovak Republic		
Slovenia		
Sweden		
United Kingdom		
Switzerland (watch cases)		
Liechtenstein (watches)		

SUMMARY

Here is a summary of *British* hallmarks including the CCM (Common Control Mark) of the *International Hallmarking Convention* and including the date letters, but excluding the national hallmarks of other countries.

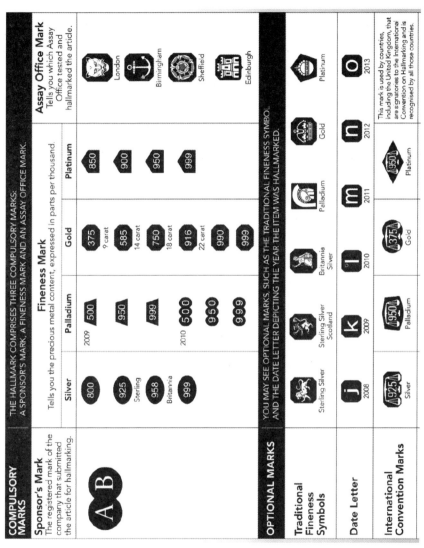

USA

Compared with the myriad of rules and regulations in Europe, the USA is very simple: there is no hallmarking, there is no national standard of testing, there is very little enforcement of mis-described items.

The best advice[1] for consumers is for 'the item's karatage [to] be identified to you in some way (verbally, through signage, etc.)' and 'If an item is stamped to indicate the quality of metal it contains, it must have a trademark in close proximity to the quality mark. (A trademark is a symbol stamped next to the quality mark and may be initials or a logo to identify the make of the item.)'

There are laws concerning the marking of gold and silver, and they date to the 1906 *National Gold and Silver Stamping Act*, but there is no national system of testing or hallmarks of any type (neither 'third party' nor 'self-certification'). In the UK if a forged mark were to be found on an item of gold, the authorities treat it as if it were forged coins or banknotes - it's serious. Not so in the USA, where 'exposures' of mis-described gold is common on TV consumer programs.

For instance:

Investigators purchased 173 suspected counterfeit items. Of these untrademarked products, 128 were found to be underkarated. The culprits were mall retailers in Arizona, California, Florida, Indiana, Louisiana, Michigan, Missouri, New Jersey, New York, North Carolina, Pennsylvania, Texas and Virginia.[2]

---

[1] This advice is from *The Jewelers Vigilance Committee*.

[2] From an undercover operation by the Jewellers Vigilance Committee, as quoted in the *Briefing Paper to the Department of Trade & Industry* by the British Hallmarking Council.

TESTING GOLD AND SILVER

MELT AND ASSAY

The most accurate method of testing gold and silver is to melt it (or, at least, melt a tiny scraping) and assay it. Bulk buyers of scrap gold will sell directly to the smelters, who will offer this service. And if you have a large amount, it might be worth paying to have it melted and assayed rather than tested by the scrap dealer. The charge for a 'gold assay' (to find out how much gold is in the alloy) is about £50.00, the charge for a 'Full Assay' which will also separate out platinum and Palladium is closer to £100.00. Once this is done you are free to choose whether to take the gold back (it will be melted into one solid lump) or sell it to the trader. Of course, if you take it back, then try to sell it to a scrap dealer another time, he will want to have it re-assayed because he won't know its composition.

As regards jewellery, melting it to find that it *was* valuable is hardly practicable and, anyway, most people merely need to know the approximate purity: 9ct or 14ct or 18ct or 22ct. Assay Offices specialise in this service (see page 16).

THE ACID TEST

The traditional test is so reliable that the term *the acid test* has entered the English language to mean *the ultimate proof.*

The principle is simple. Acid will start to dissolve 'base' metal into a vivid froth (wipe it off quickly) but will not dissolve gold or silver. Acid testers come in sets of bottles. Each bottle contains a different mixture of acid, and each mixture contains a chemical indicator that tells you the standard (purity) of the gold or silver. Although they are designed to measure the purity of gold to within 10% (accurate enough to measure the standard purities) with practice, results to within 5% accuracy are attainable[1].

Two well known brands are TROYTEST and QUICKTEST. The method is very simple: the acid is applied directly to the item, and it changes colour[2]. Unique to these brands is that the colour change is easy to see, there are even extra instructions for the colour-blind (other brands tend to turn

---

[1] For several months I kept a detailed record of every item I tested, then compared it with the 'melt and assay' result.

[2] You place the acid on the item and it is the acid that changes colour, not the item...though it can leave a dull stain behind, which must be rubbed off with a soft cloth and a jewellery polish.

green-ish or brown-ish, which all look grey to anyone who is red-green colour blind).

An alternative method of using acids (though not as simple as the QUICKTEST and TROYTEST method) is to use a touchstone (also known as a streak board). This is a small piece of slate[1] across which the test-item is drawn, so that it leaves behind a streak. Alongside this, you make a number of streaks from known samples (these come as sets of 'test needles'), you place the acid across all the streaks at once, and see which known streak dissolves (fades away) at the same rate as the unknown streak.

With *any* acid test the surface of the item must first be filed otherwise gold or silver plated items will indicate gold or silver even though the plating is very thin. That includes using a touchstone, the item *must* be filed first.

So if you ask, 'Does the acid test damage the item', the answer is yes and no. The acid doesn't damage the item (any stain can be polished off) but the file mark does...slightly. The solution is to file discreetly. I have tested several thousand items and only once was the item so intricate that there really was nowhere to file it without causing noticeable damage.

Prices of testing sets start at under £20.00 for a simple single-bottle tester to over £60.00 for a full set for testing gold, silver, platinum, palladium and Steel. Replacement bottles cost about £10.00.

Although the kits come in various combinations of bottles (and include a strong wooden box and various accessories), there are only five different mixtures of acid.

The White (9ct) Bottle

In the Troytest sets this is known as 'White Fluid', in the Quicktest set it is known as the '9ct bottle'. It is the same fluid.

Appearance: the bottle is labelled WHITE FLUID (9ct), the fluid is clear.

Purpose: to tell if a metal is not gold, or if it is 9ct, or if it is better than 9ct. If it is better than 9ct it won't tell you what it is, you must move on to the 14-24ct bottle.

.

---

[1] It doesn't have to be slate, it can be any dark acid-proof slightly rough substance, some people use bits of broken Wedgwood china.

The Blue (14-24ct) Bottle

In the Troytest sets this is known as 'Blue Fluid'. In the Quicktest set this is known as the '14ct to 24ct bottle' or the 'High carat bottle'. It is the same fluid.

Appearance: the bottle is labelled BLUE FLUID (14-24ct), the top of the cap has a blue dot (plastic bottles) or the cap is blue (glass bottles). The fluid varies from light yellow to deep yellow.

Purpose: tests for 14ct to 24ct. It is also used in combination with the GREEN fluid to distinguish WHITE gold from steel and platinum.

Tip: this fluid is to test from 14ct to 24ct having first used the 9ct fluid to test for 9ct / non-gold.

The Amber (silver) Bottle

In the Troytest sets this is known as 'Amber Fluid', in the Quicktest set it is known as the 'silver bottle', it is the same fluid.

Appearance: the bottle is labelled AMBER FLUID (silver), the top of the cap has a red dot (plastic bottles) or the cap is red (glass bottles). The colour of the fluid is amber.

Purpose: to tell if a white metal is silver, typically .925, though there's a slight reaction on silver as low as .750

The Green (platinum) Bottle
(Troytest sets only)

Appearance: the bottle is labelled GREEN FLUID, the top of the cap has a green dot (plastic bottles) or the cap is green (glass bottles). The fluid is clear.

Purpose: to differentiate 18ct WHITE gold, stainless steel and Palladium, the implication being that if it is none of these it MIGHT be platinum (unlike the other tests, this is not a 'positive' test). Most people call this the 'Platinum' bottle. HOWEVER, all these tests must be done in conjunction with the BLUE fluid, this (Green) bottle cannot be used on its own. None of this is necessary for testing yellow metals, this is only for WHITE metals.

TIP: if the metal is magnetic or if, when you file the item, you can feel that the metal is hard (as hard as the steel file) - it cannot possibly be gold or silver or platinum, there is no need to use acid. (But being magnetic does not mean it's steel, some steel is not magnetic).

The Clear (high-zinc 9ct) Bottle
(Troytest sets only)

Appearance: the bottle is labelled CLEAR FLUID (8-9ct), the top of the bottle cap has a brown dot (plastic bottles) or the cap is clear (glass bottles). The fluid is clear.

Purpose: to distinguish a particular 9ct alloy that contains a high level of zinc from 'standard' 9ct, and at the same time to give an indication of very low-grade gold such as 8ct.

Tip: this is not an easy fluid to use and should not be used in place of the standard 9ct bottle. Also, since the high-zinc alloy is quite recent, all items should be hallmarked, so test the hallmark link, check that the remainder of the item has the same reaction, and if in doubt check against a piece of copper. Only if there is *still* doubt need you use this bottle.

Observe the safety precautions: keep all bottles fastened when not in use, even between successive tests; store in a cool place, never rest a bottles on its side and *always* keep acids away from children. Work on a secure flat surface, always have a tissue to hand, to mop up any drips, and to mop up the spot after the test.

If spilt on fabric or furniture, neutralise with bicarbonate of soda, if available, and pour on plenty of water. If bicarbonate of soda is not available, don't waste time, just pour on water. Treat burns to skin by pouring on plenty of water, ideally under a running tap for at least five minutes. For details of exactly how 'dangerous' the acids are, see page 162.

Tips for Acid Testing

When first learning to use the acids, check the reaction times against pieces of gold of known purity, any hallmarked items will suffice. This should also be done to check the strength of the acids if you haven't used them for a few months. When checking against hallmarked items remember that a hallmark guarantees the purity to be at least the standard stated, it could be slightly higher.[1] Some of the sets come with a a piece of copper to test.

Always file the item with a steel file (you apply the acid to the filed area of the item not the filings) – otherwise, if the item is plated, you will merely test the gold or silver plating and that will read as 'gold' or 'silver'. Even if you are certain it isn't plated, clean the area to be tested - this is because you are observing a colour-change in the acid and you will not be able to see this against a background of dirt. If a customer forbids you to file the item, then you can't test it. However, there *will* be a place to file it discreetly - the inside of a ring shank, the back of a brooch, near the clasp of a necklace. You can even remove the rims and 'glass' from a locket to test it from the inside. Out of several thousand items I have tested there was only one occasion when I had to agree with the customer that the item was so finely made, there was nowhere 'discreet' to file it. And so I didn't buy it. If you can't file it, you can't test it.

To test high carat purity (14ct to 24ct) with acid very accurately, use a scrap British gold coin (which is exactly 916 parts per thousand): place acid on both coin and unknown gold and compare reaction times (i.e. - is the reaction on the test-item very slightly slower or very slightly faster than on the coin?)

On yellow metal it is most important to start with the 9ct bottle. This is because the 14-24ct bottle will give similar results on 9ct as it does on 14ct (and the same when used in combination with the Green fluid for testing white gold and platinum) - in other words, the results will be confusing unless you start with the 9ct bottle.

On white metal you may wish to start with the SILVER bottle instead. Usually you will know whether to test for gold or for silver, a candlestick or tray will not be gold or platinum, an intricately-made antique-looking ring with a probable diamond is not likely to be silver. But if there is doubt, start with the SILVER bottle.

---

[1] ...but not *much* higher as that would be expensive for the manufacturers.

TESTING BY FLAME

Heat the metal[1] until it goes red hot then observe the colour it turns when cooled. Fine gold (which is always bright yellow) or platinum (which is always white) will not have lost their lustre. Lower-carat gold will have become dark, with 9ct gold turning almost black and silver, too, turning black (tarnished) after the fire - they can, of course, be returned to their original shine by polishing. Steel emerges from the fire with a rainbow of colours from blue to slightly orange. You will also notice that gold and small silver items can be heated to red hot quite easily while it takes considerable effort to heat platinum or steel. Heat items gently at first, the metal may be lead which melts very easily.

TESTING BY HARDNESS

I was always fascinated, when I worked in a workshop, by one of the jewellers who would 'test' metal by filing it very gently to see how the file 'dragged'. Every jeweller soon notices that gold is very soft and that high-carat gold is very slightly softer than low-carat gold. Even a novice, with the minimum of experience, will notice that steel is so hard that the steel file seems to 'bounce' off it, and that lead is so soft it clogs up the file. This relies very much on experience, there is no machine to measure this.

TESTING WITH A MAGNET

Gold and silver are not magnetic, so if the item is magnetic it can't be gold or silver, so if you have a large number of items, start by removing anything magnetic.

'Ordinary' iron magnets cost from 50p to £5.00. Magnets made from the rare-earth element Neodymium are much more powerful[2] and they cost from £10.00 to £50.00. One advantage of a powerful magnet is that you can 'sweep' an entire bucket full of scrap in a few seconds. Another advantage is that it can pick out metals that are very very slightly magnetic, which 'ordinary' magnets will miss.

One word of warning. Steel. Some steel is magnetic and some is not.

---

[1] This should be done in the flame of a jeweller's 'torch'. The flame from a gas hob will not be powerful enough, the flame from equipment designed to weld steel can be too powerful.

[2] These are so powerful that they come with safety warnings. For instance, they can 'jump' several inches onto steel, and if your fingers happen to be in the way, they will be crushed.

ELECTRONIC TESTERS

My first project, when I went into business on my own, was the design and manufacture of a small electronic weighing balance. The project was not a success and a few years later the Japanese produced an even smaller version, and at a fraction of the price. I then got another idea. I went back to the electronics designer and said, 'Andre, I've got a brilliant idea. It will make our fortune. It would be like a thick pen into which you put a small battery. You pressed the end of the pen onto metal, and an LCD display lit up to tell you if it was gold or silver. The reading would be obtained within two or three seconds, and would also state the purity.'

'Mmmmm', said Andre, 'and how does it work?'

There was a stunned silence. '*I* don't know, I'm just the inventor, *you* have to design it!'

In the end, we didn't come up with a design. Someone else did. Their electronic gold tester (the very first) came onto the market in 1987 and I immediately started selling them. What happened next was very interesting, and I had a similar experience recently when testing the very latest x-ray (XRF) testers.

The very first production batch (this was in 1987) was split between myself and a London wholesaler. I, cautiously, bought three and the wholesaler bought ten.

After a few weeks, all three of mine had been returned. They were inaccurate. There followed many protracted conversations between myself, the importer and the manufacturer. Nobody else, said the importer, had any problems...the machines were guaranteed accurate to within ½ carat. Eventually I proved beyond doubt that the machines were faulty and the manufacturers grudgingly admitted that *all* the machines were faulty. Yet there were no complaints from the wholesaler who sold to shopkeepers, only from my own customers in the antiques trade. Why?

This is my theory:

In a jewellery shop a member of public offers an item to sale. Either it is hallmarked, in which case it does not need testing; or it is not. The shopkeeper then tests the item on his new electronic gold tester. This impresses both customer and shopkeeper, both are convinced that modern technology must give a more accurate answer than acids; *and* the customer can see a light on machine - he doesn't have to rely on the shopkeepers word. The result: if the machine indicates 14ct on a typically 15ct Victorian item, the shopkeeper will pay as if it were 14ct, and if the machine indicates 12ct the shopkeeper will pay accordingly. If the item is scrap the shopkeeper will probably not even notice the discrepancy (and if he does he may keep quiet), if the item is saleable it will be sold as the lower carat. The customer will never return to query the accuracy of the machine.

The scenario is very different in the antiques trade, into which I was selling these machines.

A trader buys a piece of jewellery from another trader as 'unmarked but tested with acid and guaranteed 9ct'. The buyer tests the item on the machine and the machine reads only '8ct'. There is then a dispute between the two traders. After three or four such disputes, the owner of the electronic gold tester becomes suspicious and double-checks the readings against acids. Eventually there is no doubt - the tester is not as accurate as a traditional set of acids.

LOW-COST PORTABLE ELECTRONIC TESTERS

Although brands come and go, there only seem to be three on the market at the time of going to press, and all three are from the USA. This is not, of course, to say that a better model isn't about to hit the market. In fact, I am trying to design my own, but so far I'm having difficulty in 'inventing' one that is better than all the others currently on the market, but I live in hope that there will soon be a breakthrough[1].

Mizar

The approximate price range (there are various models) is £100.00 to £150.00. The method is as follows.

Clean a small area of the item with the eraser (a simple pencil rubber), fill the 'well' (a hollow in the machine) with 'activator fluid' (acid) from a small bottle, clip part of the item to the crocodile clip, then dip another part of

---

[1] Contact raffi@quicktest.co.uk

the item very carefully into the fluid without it touching the sides of the 'well'. Lights indicate the purity (carat).

If you suspect the item might be heavily gold plated you must varnish a small area of the item. File through the varnish into the item with a steel file, put the acid over the varnish / filed area, test it, clean everything up thoroughly, test it again on a non-varnished / non-filed area, then compare the two readings, a laborious process.

So how do you know whether to test just the surface or test it for plating? Answer: you don't. That's why you're testing it.

After each test you must meticulously clean out the 'well' (the indentation you fill with acid) otherwise the acid will corrode and destroy the machine. Most people don't spend enough time cleaning out the 'well' and after a few months it corrodes and the machine stops working...and is not covered by the guarantee...and is not worth repairing.

As for the accuracy, the top model has lights to indicate 9ct, 10ct, 12ct, 14ct, 16ct, 18ct, 20ct, 22ct, 24ct. Since you never know if the machine is rounding the reading up or down, you will only ever know the answer to the nearest 4ct, and by that standard (about 15%) it is accurate, but of no use if the item is plated.

They do not test for silver or platinum.

Tri Electronics

These are much more sophisticated than the Mizar, though more expensive, ranging (there are various models) from £200.00 to £500.00.

The basic principle is the same as the Mizar, you clip one part of the object to a crocodile clip, use an acid as a contact fluid (though it's dispensed as a gel from a special 'pen' rather than just dripped out of a bottle) and read the answer on the display. This one comes with a useful CD containing a video, so that you can see what is involved in real time, and this also shows you that testing an item takes between five and seven minutes. I shan't describe the process, you must read their 20-page instruction manual.

The top model is impressive in that the purity is displayed very precisely (in either carat or parts per thousand) on an LCD display, and it also tests platinum.

As for the accuracy, it does seem to correctly identify platinum every time, 22ct is accurate to within 5% (comparable with acid testers). As for 9ct to 18ct, the readings *look* wildly inaccurate because the parts per thousand on the display appear far removed from reality, but when we do the arithmetic we find it is accurate to within 10%, better than the Mizar but not as good as acids. The only annoying part is that you have to spend 3 or 4 minutes cleaning the dispenser every few tests, and you do have to carry out 3 or 4 tests on each item because some readings are totally wrong. That's why it takes so long to test each item.

They do not test for silver.

Golden Touch

Unlike the other electronic testers, there is no acid involved no filing of the items involved, it is totally safe, totally non-destructive, and it's not expensive. The method of testing is very simple indeed, you 'draw' the sample across a strip of wet paper, turn a knob, and observe the colour of the streak on the paper.

The sample we bought was so inaccurate it was totally useless. Just to check that this wasn't a faulty machine (or an early model) I bought another one a couple of years later, with the same result.

Our own technician says that this machine cannot possibly work, because the result depends on the area of metal drawn across the paper, the speed at which you move it and the amount of pressure you apply. And that assumes you can 'grade' the carat from the colour chart provided.

XRF (WDX) ELECTRONIC TESTERS

CABINET-TYPE

This is X-ray Fluorescence (Wavelength Dispersive) technology; it uses an x-ray tube similar to those that take x-rays of broken bones. What you get is a cabinet the size of a microwave oven, it connects to a computer, you place the sample inside and lock the door firmly (the x-rays are dangerous) and within a minute or two an analysis of the precious metal content appears on the computer screen. The price of these at the moment is £8,000.00 to £10,000.00.

Pros

Flexible computer-controlled analysis - but I've never actually used one of these so I can't tell you about the ease of use or accuracy of results.

Cons

The following is what I have gleaned from prolonged correspondence with an overseas manufacture. I have not had a chance to play with one of these machines.

Learning to use acids will only take a few minutes; an XRF requires proper 'training' in how to use both the machine and the software. This is one of the reasons these machines tend to be expensive, because 'training' is included in the price[1]. Physically placing the sample on the test-plate and pressing some buttons is not difficult, but 'filters' have to be set up to test for specific metals, you need to learn how to use the computer software, it helps to know about spectrography and understand graphs.

Unlike simpler testers there are a dozen things that can go wrong, and then you have to systematically check both the electrics, the software, and your testing method to track down the fault.

It's slow compared with a standard acid test. An acid test will take 5 seconds to open the box and bottle, 5 seconds to file the item, 2 seconds to apply the acid, 3 to 30 seconds to note the reaction, 5 seconds to carefully mop up the residue...add up the numbers, it's quick.

An XRF cabinet is not so quick. When you start up the machine at the beginning of the day it takes 20 minutes to warm up (during which time you can also start up the computer and software), you must check the calibration, you must be slow and careful about setting up the sample in the machine, there might even be a CCTV camera in the machine to help you; a 'quick' test for precious metals then takes a minute or two; a 'complete' test of all metals in the sample can take ten or fifteen minutes. This is too slow if you have a busy shop with customers queuing, or a dealer with a 'parcel' of a hundred items each weighing a couple of grams.

---

[1] If you buy one as a 'bargain' from overseas, you will not get the support, neither advice nor servicing nor spare parts.

XRF, HANDHELD TYPE

The market leader in this sector is the family of Thermo Scientific Niton handheld XRF analysers.[1] Their instruments are the size of a barcode scanner, feature a built-in touch-screen, and are totally self-contained (power is from a rechargeable battery). Prices start at £14,500.00.[2]

Pros

No calibration is required other than selecting, 'Precious Metals' from the menu on the touch-screen, all the necessary processing technology is built into the instrument.

Testing is fast. For a very approximate analysis one five second press of the trigger will suffice; generally you would take four or five readings and press the 'average' button; if you get inconsistent readings you need to take longer (eg. 30 second) tests for greater accuracy; if you have a large totally unknown item (eg. a bar) you may wish to test it in several places. Whatever the degree of testing, it *will* be faster than the same degree of testing with acids and *much* faster than other electronic testers.

On the screen you see a chart, the first column shows the name (chemical symbol) of the metal, the second column calculates the percentage present in the sample, a third column gives the percentage accuracy for that test - no reading will ever be 100% accurate but overall it *should* be five to ten times more accurate than acids.

The instrument also keeps a record of all tests made, either for immediate reference or to download onto a computer.

You can scan a bag full of small bits of scrap. As you scan, the machine registers the surface of the nearest items and gives an average for the lot.

Cons

At nearly £15,000.00 it is quite expensive. Also, the x-ray tube doesn't last forever (it should last about five years) and replacements cost £4,000.00.

Each user has to enter a PIN code to use the machine, which should minimise the risk of a customer picking it up and pressing the trigger, but

---

[1] Thermo Scientific Niton handheld analysers are produced by Thermo Fisher Scientific Inc, and are available in the UK only through authorised distributors Niton UK Limited, see www.nitonuk.co.uk

[2] The model we tested was XL2. Thermo also sell obsolete models (reconditioned) for £10,000.00.

the x-rays *are* highly dangerous if pointed directly at somebody.

The x-rays penetrate between 5µ and 6µ.[1] That presents no problem with most plating but heavily-plated items will fool the machine. Although *the* feature of these instruments is that it is non-destructive, our 20µ-plated item showed up as 14ct gold (with 1% zinc content), we should have filed it first. You do also need to make sure the item is clean, we got misleading readings when testing dirty gold.[2]

Pros *and* Cons

A rolled gold item gave various readings from 9ct to 18ct (and a high zinc content), an example of why it is wise to take a few readings. It is simply not good enough to carry out one test, glance at the screen and come to a conclusion, you must combine your scrap-buying experience with a little knowledge of chemistry. This will help avoid expensive mistakes and will provide a huge amount of extra information. Here are some examples:

An old pendant was giving various (low) readings for gold and a consistently high reading for silver, it was silver gilded with gold. A more detailed analysis showed a trace of mercury. This indicated that it had been mercury gilded.[3]

A nice quality bracelet, heavy and with a handmade catch and safety clip (a typical high-quality gold item) showed only 3% gold, 44% copper and 40% nickel. In this case the item did not need filing (to get below the plating), it was obviously not gold, the 3% being a very thin layer of plating, the nickel being used to help the plating process.

A impressive gold coloured coin (and you would *never* want to file a collector's coin) showed copper, tin and manganese (manganese-bronze) and no gold at all; a sample of Palladium contained Gallium which suggested it was intended as a dental alloy rather than for making jewellery; a silver pendant contained cadmium which produces toxic fumes when melted (smelters don't like that); a yellow and white ring was 22ct but with 0.2% rhodium which showed that the white part of the ring was rhodium plating (rhodium plating is rarely more than 1µ thick).

---

[1]   µ (micron) = 1 / 1000mm

[2]   To be more technical, it had 'surface contamination' though we've no idea what this was. A firm polish with fine emery paper was good enough to shine it up and remove the contamination.

[3]   Gold would be mixed with mercury then the mercury burnt off. The resulting fumes are highly toxic, leading to neurological problems such as loss of sight, hearing and speech, plus impaired coordination and death. The process is not used any more. Mercury was also used for making felt for hats, hence the saying, "As mad as a hatter."

OTHER ELECTRONIC TESTERS

Whilst XRF has moved from 'too expensive' to 'affordable for a company', other technology is still in its infancy, for instance, ICP.[1] To illustrate this, I quote from the 'chat' emails of the Gemmological Association of Great Britain, someone asked if these various testers, used for metals, can also be used for gemstones. The response (from user 'Bear') discusses the relative merits of these technologies:

> From what I've gathered, the overlap problem is something akin to the grating problem with spectrometers. In the case of XRF, as the X-ray source excites the sample, you will have a signature overlap based on how atoms are stacked. The energy released from the test sample may have a similar emission based on its electron configuration. But yes, you can use just one instrument to get all your readings. These problems have been overcome by using a multi-channel type system that eliminates the overlap...you just have to pay more for it. There is another method called WDX that works in similar fashion to XRF but (I believe) it manipulates the emission and re-interprets in waves.

My point is that only the largest of organisations (eg. The Assay Office) can afford these at the moment.

TESTING - HINTS AND TIPS

Look before you test! Often the name of the metal is clearly visible. Learn to recognise hallmarks and also the marks of *the International Hallmarking Convention* (used by 19 countries). A hallmarked item need not be tested, though you may wish to test anything which involves large amounts of money. Forged hallmarks do exist but they are rare, forgers are discouraged by the prospect of up to seven years' imprisonment. If you are not sure if you have a genuine hallmark, ask any jeweller; if you *are* a jeweller, ask at any assay office, they will verify its authenticity free of charge, or will start investigations if it is a forgery.[2]

Use a magnifier that you get on with. Some people can only see well through weak magnifiers, some through strong magnifiers. If lighting is a problem, buy a magnifier with a built-in light, it makes all the difference.

---

[1] Inductively-coupled plasma mass spectrometry. It requires high-vacuum system, high energy electron beam and an X-ray detector.

[2] One jeweller sent some imported jewellery for hallmarking, and when it failed the 18ct test and was marked 14ct he filled in the hallmarks with solder and sent them to another assay office 'for a second opinion'. For this minor tampering with a hallmark he was fined £1500.00. Another jeweller 'copied' antique silver items complete with forged silver marks and was sentenced to three years' imprisonment under the Forgery Act 2008.

Gold of 22ct to 24ct is always yellow. Lower-carat gold can be yellow, red, pink or white. Silver and platinum are always white.

Gold, silver and platinum are not magnetic. A magnet is not, however, a test for steel since not all steel is magnetic.

Gold, silver and platinum are soft compared with steel, you will notice the moment you try to file it. Similarly, lead is so soft that it instantly clogs the file (and can be cut with a penknife). Gold, silver and platinum are heavy (as is lead).

Some clues can be gained from stone-set jewellery. Diamonds are usually set in 18ct gold, sometimes in 9ct gold but very rarely in 'base' metals; paste (glass) is not set into 18ct gold and rarely in 9ct gold [1].

Some metals are distinctive in themselves. Steel has a harsh lustre due to its hardness and scratch-resistance. Brass, copper and chrome have distinctive colours too (though 9ct gold containing copper also looks coppery). Lead has a dull sheen and a characteristic muddy colour when old. Aluminium is very light in weight.

Take extra care with large items made out of sheets of gold or silver, they are filled with wax or lead to make them heavier, eg. silver cigar boxes, candlesticks and anything marked 'gold cased'. A good formula for calculating the weight is: cubic area in centimetres X 0.007 (the answer is approximate).

On B&F (Back & Front, see page 15): the back and the front the locket are gold but the rims, catches, frames, loop and jump ring are not. The weight of gold is less than half a gram but they are saleable when in complete and in good condition (inside the locket there should be rims holding in glass or Perspex, under which can be a photograph and lock of hair).

RG (rolled gold, see page 15): bangles tend to be 'springy' when bent whereas gold will remain in its new position. RG watch cases were guaranteed to last twenty or thirty years and this guarantee is proudly engraved into the metal, GUARANTEED TO WEAR 20 YEARS - your guarantee that the item is not gold. In the USA the GUARANTEED TO WEAR 20 YEAR

---

[1] There are, of course, exceptions. cubic zirconia can be set in 18ct, diamonds can be set in 'base' metal which has been rhodium plated to look like 18ct white gold or platinum.

notice was eventually abolished. Since the layer of gold (often 14ct) can be as thick as the non-gold, the only way to test it is to file a deep notch before applying acid.

Even solid gold and silver items can be plated, sometimes by the manufacturer and sometimes by a workshop following a repair. 9ct gold is plated with 18ct or 22ct and white gold is plated with rhodium, in both cases to improve the colour. Silver can be plated with rhodium or palladium to prevent tarnishing. Even if you are certain that the item you are testing is gold it is still wise to file it before carrying out an acid test.

Hollow gold is solid gold filled with air, traditionally gold tubing, though modern techniques enable nearly any shape to be made hollow. This is to economise on the weight of gold (usually 9ct but sometimes 14ct or 18ct) and looks just like the solid equivalent. The disadvantage of hollow gold is that it is difficult or impossible to repair - you may have more luck reassembling a squashed insect than repairing a squashed hollow gold bangle.

The following are not gold: the mechanisms in propelling pencils and sprung lids, the springs in expanding watch bracelets, watch cases with steel backs, the springy arms of old spectacles, most pen nibs, the gold coloured paint used on furniture.

Old dental plates and gold caps vary between 16ct and 20ct. Pen nibs are 14ct only if marked as such. 22ct gold or higher can only be bright yellow in colour, the colour of lower carats varies.

Silver plate is easily confused with solid silver. Very often the dull 'base' metal can be seen through worn silver plating but tarnished silver can have the same appearance. Plated items can be collectable *providing* the plating is not wearing off. Silversmiths once registered plate marks at the Sheffield Assay Office - the marks can be found at the back of *Dealer Guides, English Silver Hallmarks by Judith Banister.*[1]

There is also an international book of hallmarks by Tardy.[2] Not only does the Tardy contain over 500 pages of marks from around the world, but there's an ingenious index at the back which is in *picture order* so that you can look up a mark without knowing the country.

---

[1] available from QUICKTEST, www.quicktest.co.uk.

[2] Although referred to, in the trade, simply as "Tardy" its full name is *International Hallmarks on Silver collected by Tardy. It is available from* QUICKTEST (www.quicktest.co.uk)

THE GOLD AND SILVER PRICE

Twice a day, at 10.30am and 3pm, five men would gather in an office at Rothschilds. Each man represents a bullion bank (Rothschild, Sharps Pixley, Mocatta & Goldsmid, Johnson Matthey and Samuel Montagu) and they would decide the price of gold.

Exactly the same happens today, except that it's all done on a conference call rather than having to physically meet, and today the five are: The Bank of Nova Scotia, HSBC, Deutsche Bank AG London, Societe Generale Corporate & Investment Banking and Barclays Capital.[1]

One of them (the Chairman) announces an opening price to the other four who relay the price to their customers, and based on orders received from them, declare themselves *buyers* or *sellers* at that price, and state the amount of gold they wish to trade. Since it's unlikely that they will all be in agreement, the price has to be adjusted and the procedure repeated until the buy-amount and the sell-amount are the same.[2] The chairman then declares that the price is 'fixed' for the morning (or afternoon), and this is the 'middle' price between buying and selling - the 'official' price of gold for the morning (or afternoon), the *actual gold price*. The process takes just a few minutes.[3]

'The fix' is the 'official' price of gold at approximately 10.30am and 3pm each working day, it is a good price to quote when someone says, 'What is the price of gold today?' - but since gold (as with every other commodity) is traded on the international markets, the price will change, and it will change from minute to minute.

Trading in gold never stops. Soon after the London market closes at 4.30pm trading starts in New York; then as New York prices vanish from the screens (at 7.30pm GMT) trading has started in Hong Kong. The gold price will 'open' in London in line with the last ('closing') Hong Kong price, which would have followed that of New York, which, in turn, would have opened in line with London's closing price.

So how much is gold worth?

---

[1] Sharps Pixley were acquired by Deutsche Bank AG; NM Rothschilds & Sons Ltd sold their Fixing Seat to Barclays; Mocatta & Goldsmid were taken over by Bank of Nova Scotia; Samuel Montagu were taken over by Midland (now HSBC). As for the Johnson Matthey seat, it went first to Mace Westpac, then to Republic National Bank, then to Credit Suisse and finally to Societe General

[2] It's sufficient for them to agree to the nearest 50 bars of gold

[3] ...though on one occasion, in 1990, it took over two hours

The price of one ounce of pure (24ct) gold varies. it varies over the years, it varies over the months and weeks, and it varies from minute to minute. And it varies quite a lot:

1660		£	4.05
1815		£	5.35
1900	$ 20.67	£	4.94
1954	$ 35.00	£	12.42
1971	$ 41.00	£	16.50
1979	$ 850.00	£340.00	
1999	$ 152.00	£	96.00
2009	$1200.00	£745.00[1]	

Since the price is quoted in US Dollars, the price in Pounds Sterling also fluctuates with the exchange rate. And since the price bobs up and down so much, anyone who wants to persuade you that gold is a good investment can pick figures to suit.

The price of gold is quoted in dollars per ounce. This is for pure gold. To find the pure gold weight of jewellery and coins use FORMULA B on page 47. To convert dollars to pounds sterling divide by the exchange rate (the 'cable'). The following chart, from Kitco, shows prices from 2000 to 2010.

---

[1] Allowing for inflation this isn't as high as in 1979

The latest gold and silver prices can be found on the financial news on the radio and television, the financial pages of daily newspapers, and, of course, the internet. To avoid millions of 'hits' that have no relevance to the *actual* gold price, search the internet for *Current Gold Price*. The official website for the gold fix is www.goldfixing.com. Apart from that, top of the charts at the moment are: www.kitco.com, www.goldprice.org, www.goldpricetoday.co.uk and www.goldprices.com.

So why *does* the price of gold vary so much. There are many factors:

Supply and demand (eg. governments selling gold reserves) or gold-producers cutting back on production; laws preventing people buying or exporting gold or currencies; political factors including the threat of war (in the Middle East this leads to rising oil price rises and more political and economic instability); the effect of natural disasters (eg. hurricanes damaging oil rigs); other technical factors such as refineries shut down for maintenance; other political factors such as unstable governments (economists worry about their ability to control the economy); other economic factors such as inflation, banking crises, stock market crashes, property slumps etc.

Even when the dollar price of gold remains stable, the local price may change. In the immediate aftermath of the May 2010 general election, with no one party in overall control, the strength of the pound weakened against the dollar, making gold more expensive in pounds (the pound strengthened as soon as a government was formed).

When people lose faith in 'paper' wealth they turn to 'things. e.g. property (not much good if there's a property slump) or works of art (easily damaged and their value is subject to the whims of collectors)...or gold.

Here is a selection of events that led to the gold boom of 1979-1980.

1972 Lowest price, this year, was $44.00

1972 Average price for the year, $58.00
The USSR and South Africa temporarily stop selling gold, leading to a speculative boom. Price rises to $69.00 upon a rumour that Europe will use a price higher than the official $38.00 for valuing their gold reserves.

1974 Average price for the year, $159.00
French government resigns, monetary policy tightened, Soviet gold sales curtailed, oil prices quadruple, US inflation doubles.

1975 Average price for the year, $161.00
US lifts restriction on members of the public owning gold and holds its first gold auctions, but only manages to sell half the gold they had hoped. G10 decides not to increase the amount of gold held by the IMF and other monetary authorities, and then to sell 50 million ounces.

1978 Average price for the year,$193.00
US sells more of its gold reserves, fear about rising inflation, heavy buying of gold by Middle East investors.

1979 Average price for the year $305.00
War in the Middle East, USA ends its gold auctions, the Iranian revolution followed by the return of Khomeini, then the USA cuts diplomatic relations with Iran, then the Iranian Hostage Crisis.

1980 Highest price, this year, was $850.00
The USSR invasion of Afghanistan (they actually invaded on 25 December 1979), USA makes an abortive attempt to rescue the Iranian hostages, Iraq invades Iran (the first Gulf War), oil prices rise, inflation rises, jewellery demand drops.

The price then fell, reaching a low of $255.00 in 2001, then climbed to over $1000.00 in 2009.

Prices vary slightly from minute to minute. The prices given on the radio and television can be a few hours out of date and those shown in a morning newspaper will be nearly a day out of date. If, however, you are buying or selling small amounts the actual difference in money between one day and the next *probably* won't be great.

All this explains why it was, when I was silly enough to start a discussion with a bullion dealer about the gold price, his response, 'It is not for us to question why, it is for us to sell and buy.'

The 'current gold price' (from websites that have no interest in actually buying your gold) will be the 'spot' price, the 'on the spot' price at a particular moment - but you will never get this much when selling scrap. Generally, expect between 50% and 75% for small quantities (a few hundred pounds); up to 90% for large quantities (a few thousand pounds) and up to 98% for very large quantities (tens of thousands of pounds).
Use the formula on page 47, to calculate prices.

Details of how much to expect can be found in the chapter *BUYING AND SELLING* from page 73.

FORMULAE FOR CALCULATING PRICES

Quick Method to find the actual gold value:

- Look up the price per ounce (which is always given in US Dollars)
- Convert to Pounds Sterling by dividing by the exchange rate
- Divide the answer by 31.1035 to get the price per gram
- Multiply the answer by .375 for 9ct or .585 for 14ct or .750 for 18ct or .916 for 22ct. If you have gold of a 'non standard' purity (eg. from outside the U.K) use Formula A below.

This is the price per gram, weigh the gold in grams. If you shortcut the system by weighing in ounces, make sure you switch your weighing machine to **Troy** ounces (about 31g) not Avoirdupois ounces, which is used for weighing food (about 28g).

Quick Method for silver:

Look up the price, if you are using a UK website the price will be in British Pounds per ounce, if your weighing machine can be switched to ounces (**Troy** Ounces, not the *Avoirdupois* ounce used for weighing food) you shouldn't need a formula to work out the price. If your weighing machine can't be switched to ounces or, more likely, you leave it permanently set to grams, divide by 31.1035 to get Troy Ounces.

FORMULA *A*:

PARTS PER THOUSAND AND CARAT

Carat ÷ 24 X 1000 = parts per thousand
eg. 9ct. ÷ 24 X 1000 = 375 parts per thousand

Parts per thousand ÷ 1000 x 24 = carat
eg. 375 ÷ 1000 X 24 = 9ct.

FORMULA *B*:

31.1034g = 1oz. So divide ounces by 31.1035[1].

---

[1] More accurately, 31.1034768, but 31.1035 is good enough

FORMULA C:

PURE SILVER/GOLD WEIGHT FROM GROSS WEIGHT

Parts per thousand X gross weight ÷ 1000 = net weight
eg. 375 X 1.5oz. ÷ 1000 = 0.5625oz. of pure gold

FORMULA D:

'X FACE VALUE' OF SILVER COINS (BRITISH) FROM SILVER PRICE PER OUNCE

'Spot' silver price per oz. X purity X 3.5527
eg. £5 per oz. X 0.5 (Pre-1947 coins[1]) x 3.5527 = £8.88
(Rate realised, between 60% and 80% of this figure)

FORMULA E:

THE VALUE OF GOLD PLATING

Area in mm X thickness in mm ÷ 1000 x 19.32^2 = pure gold in grams.

eg. for a bangle with plating thickness of 1.5μ (=0.0015mm)
and surface area of 10mm x 5mm x 2 sides:

10 x 5 x 2 ÷ 1000 x 19.32 x 0.0015
= 0.0029 grams of pure gold.[3]

Of this 70 to 80% will be reclaimable. Value of gold: about 5p.

The thickness of the gold plating on electronic circuit boards varies from 10μ on modern boards to 25μ on old boards; ordinary costume jewellery varies from 5μ to 10μ; very good quality costume jewellery and cigarette lighters, up to 30μ. A plating thickness of 6μ should last 5 years; 12μ, 10 years, 18μ, 15 years and 24μ, 20 years before wearing off.

---

[1] For coins dated before 1920 multiply by 0.925 instead of 0.500.

[2] 19.32 is the specific density of gold.

[3] This assumes that pure gold is used for plating, often the quality of the plating is 18ct - see formula C.

WEIGHTS, GOLD AND MONEY

Gold and silver were once the currency of the world. In the Middle Ages 'travellers' (traders) would visit towns and villages and would carry scales with them to weigh the silver they were paid. Small items would be paid for in copper. The original copper penny weighed 1oz, twelve of which could be exchanged for a silver shilling. The Industrial Revolution brought with it spending power for the masses but great poverty too. Workers who could not even afford to deal in pennies would be paid in smaller copper tokens which could be spent in the factory shop or exchanged for the large copper penny. Copper was the currency of the masses, silver was the currency of the small trader, gold was the currency of property deals, imports and exports. This three tier currency system (copper, silver, gold) lasted until 1972 when Britain changed to a decimal system of coinage.

By 1972 few people remembered - or cared - that the world's economy was once based on weights of gold and silver. Silver had not been used for making circulation coins in Britain since 1946 and gold had not been used as everyday currency since the 1910s. Gold and silver values, however, are still based on weight - all such items start life as molten metal and most end their life back in the melting pot, even antique items are melted if the gold value rises much above the aesthetic value. From smelter and bullion house to manufacturer and wholesaler and back to scrap merchant and smelter, all values are based upon weight. Unless, of course, the main value is in precious stones or because the item is antique and rare. These exceptions aside, it is only in the high street shop that 'fashion value' far exceeds gold value[1]. The most important piece of equipment for the gold and silver buyer, apart from a set of testing acids, is a set of weighing scales.

---

[1] For those who only buy gold as jewellery from high street jewellery shops, it is a sobering thought that the value of the gold in new jewellery is only about 20% of the retail price.

WEIGHTS AND WEIGHING

A BRIEF HISTORY OF WEIGHTS

Fine gold or fine silver has a value relative to its weight. Purity can be tested anywhere in the world by anyone who has a selection of acids and some simple instructions. No instructions, no matter how complex, can be used to describe a unit of weight. Weight cannot be defined in terms of natural standards, the only way to decide upon an exact standard of weight is physically to make one. *The* standard kilogram weight is kept in the offices of the International Bureau of Weights and Measures in Paris, it is made out of a lump of platinum iridium. All other Kilogram weights are based on this sample.

It was only recently that the kilogram was adopted as the standard unit of weight. Other systems of weights were, and still are, used.

Fifteenth-century Europe used an ingenious standard which, though not accurate by today's standards, was adequate: a grain of wheat. The unit was called a grain (gr.). For heavier objects the pound was used. This was where the confusion began. There was no standard pound. In fact, there were six different pounds and each weighed a different number of grains.

Henry VIII (1509 to 1547) tidied the system just a little. He introduced a standard pound of 5760 grains for weighing coins. This was the Troy pound, already common in much of Europe (it possibly originated in the French town of Troyes). This was greatly satisfying for the King but did not impress the people who continued to use other pounds. Queen Elizabeth (1558 to 1603) introduced another standard pound for the weighing of food and goods, the Avoirdupois Pound which weighed 7000 grains (*avoirdupois* means *goods of weight* in old French).

It was George III (1727 to 1760) who decided that there should be only one standard pound. He chose to 'standardise' the existing Troy pound, still in use for weighing coins, by manufacturing an exact Troy pound weight (5760 grains) for all other weights to be based upon. This was to be the new Imperial standard. Alas, disaster struck. First the King died, which delayed implementation until 1824, then, in 1834, the 'master' weight was destroyed in a fire. The people, by now used to the Avoirdupois pound, showed no interest in changing. Parliament bowed to public opinion and decided to officially adopt the Avoirdupois pound. So it was then that scientists manufactured an exact Avoirdupois pound weight (7000 grains).

There were now just two systems of weights: Troy (for coins) and Avoirdupois (for goods, including food). This meant that unscrupulous traders could deceive the public by using the wrong pound. This last inconsistency was cured in 1878 when all reference to the Troy pound was forbidden. The Troy system is still used today for weighing precious metals but the highest unit is the ounce and not the pound. The ounce and the pound of the Avoirdupois system are also used today - for weighing food and goods. It is important, therefore, to remember that we still use two different ounces, the Troy ounce is for weighing gold and silver, the Avoirdupois ounce is the 'kitchen scales' ounce.

THE TROY, AVOIRDUPOIS AND METRIC SYSTEMS

The jewellery trade once used the Troy system: grains, pennyweights and ounces. Today the metric system presides: gold is always weighed in grams and silver prices are sometimes quoted per kilogram.[1] This is most inconvenient because the basic price of gold and silver is still quoted in Troy ounces. To make matters worse, the novice weighs gold and silver on his kitchen scales and wonders why his local jeweller suddenly doesn't seem to understand 'ordinary' pounds and ounces.

This is the troy system of weights:

24 grains (gr.)	= 1 Pennyweight (DWT)[2]
20 DWT	= 1 ounce (oz)
12 oz	= 1 pound (lb) - BANNED SINCE 1878

This is the metric system of weights:

100 points = 1 carat[3]
  5 carats = 1 gram (g)
1000 grams= 1 kilogram (Kg)
1000 Kg   = 1 tonne

There is also a metric grain used for weighing diamonds, 4 gr = 1 carat.

This is how gold and silver is weighed today, metric *and* troy:

31.1 grams = 1 ounce
32.2 ounces = 1 Kilogram

An important number to remember is 31.1 (to be more exact, 31.1035), it is the key to all grams/ounces and ounces/grams conversions. Few people today use grains and pennyweights. Those who do will find it helpful to remember two more conversions:

Pennyweight X 1.555 = grams
Grams   X 0.646 = Pennyweight

---

[1] Except in the USA where ounces and pennyweight are still used

[2] The 'd' is from the Latin *denarius* and 'wt' is for *weight*

[3] Used for weighing precious stones, especially diamonds. 1 carat = $^1/_{150}$th oz. Carat weight should not be confused with carat purity (and in the USA carat, as a purity, is spelled karat).

Kitchen scales weigh in ounces Avoirdupois:

16oz = 1 pound

(Once grains were used too: 437½gr. = 1oz, 7,000gr. = 1lb. These are no longer used)

If only kitchen scales are available deduct 10% from the weight to get an approximate answer in Troy ounces. Spring-loaded scales are not very accurate, especially kitchen scales which are not designed for weighing very light objects. The pan-and-weights scale (the beam balance) is more accurate though the smallest kitchen weight is likely to be ¼oz. Providing a kitchen beam balance is sensitive enough (see section on weighing) it is well worth buying a set of jewellers' gram weights down to ½ gram. All gram weights are the same, whether used for weighing precious metals or food.

One last variation is worthy of mention. Apothecaries' weights were Troy ounces but each ounce was divided into 8 drachms and each drachm into 60 grains (i.e. the same 5760 grains as the Troy ounce but the middle unit, instead of the pennyweight, is the drachm). Today pharmacists use the metric system.

CONVERSIONS

1 ozT (Troy oz) =	0.911 oz	Avoirdupois oz
	31.1035 g	grams
	20 dwt	pennyweight
	480 gr	grains

1 dwt (pennyweight) = 1.555g.

1 Kg (Kilogram)   = 32.151 Troy oz

1lb (Pound)   = 14.576 Troy oz = 453.37g

THE LAW CONCERNING WEIGHING

The Basics

Any apparatus used for weighing must be approved by the Trading Standards Department *if it is to be used for trade*. Approved weights and scales are stamped with a crown and a date letter. Weights & Measures Inspectors tour the country checking that only approved instruments are used and that they are in good working order.

Many people become very worried when they hear they can be prosecuted for using unapproved weighing machines. The law only applies to weighing machines in 'USE FOR TRADE'. If you are not buying or selling you may weigh goods on anything. I quote from the WEIGHTS AND MEASURES ACT 1985 (Part 2, section 7):

> *An approved weighing machine must be used when 'the transaction is by reference to quantity'* [i.e. buying or selling on a value-for-weight basis] *or is a transaction for the purposes of which there is made or implied a statement of the quantity of goods to which the transaction relates* [i.e. even if you pre-weigh the goods or pre-calculate the price by weight, you must use an approved weighing machine].

What does this mean in practice? A trader may use a non-approved weighing machine for his own information providing he is not buying and selling on a weight basis. So if he is buying or selling an antique diamond ring and wants an indication of weight it is quite permissible to weigh it on an unapproved instrument, calculate the value of the stones then calculate the antique or fashion value. In theory, a trader can be prosecuted for simply *possessing* an unapproved weighing machine on trade premises and if the offending machine was not for trade use it is for the trader to prove this to a court. In practice, Weights & Measures Inspectors visit shops posing as customers, they can then see for themselves how prices are calculated. These rules apply whether trading is between trader and public or purely within the trade.

If you set up a stall in a street market one Saturday and buy or sell gold or silver by weight, then you are a trader (even if you are an insurance broker or a dock worker for the rest of the week) and you *could* be prosecuted. You are even a trader if you hold a jewellery party at home for your friends and buy or sell by weight...but Weights & Measures Inspectors have enough work to do without having to visit private homes.

At antiques fairs and markets, all silver dealers, antique jewellery dealers, and scrap and bullion merchants use spring balances or miniature digital balances to help them buy and sell. Sometimes the calculations are a private and somewhat secret affair and only final prices are quoted, sometimes trading is quite openly on a price-per-ounce or price-per-gram basis. The law, outlined above, still applies, but traders ignore it. They buy amongst themselves and they must make quick decisions based on quick weighing. This is not, of course, to say that the law can safely be ignored forever, one day there *will* be a clamp-down.

Auction houses do not need to use approved balances. They may be using a balance to help value items according to the weight of precious metal, but they are not actually buying or selling anything, they are merely carrying out a valuation to set a reserve price - it is the bidders who will be buying.

Pawnbroking is a dubious area. On the one hand, as with auctioning, balances are used to value items for the purposes of lending money, not actually buying or selling. On the other hand, most of the time the value *will* be entirely on a price-per-weight basis. At the moment (2010) if you contact your local trading standards department about this, they are likely to say they don't know the answer.

The Details

Who 'approves' the balances? Who enforces the law?

The actual standards for Weights and Measures are determined by the National Weights & Measures Laboratory who study the law, look at the science, and issue guidelines to Weights & Measures Authorities. But here's the catch. Each Local Council's Trading Standards department has its own interpretation of the law. I will try to clarify the rules but at the end of the day you might have to revert to telephoning them.

The law is enforced by Weights and Measures inspectors, they work for the Trading Standards department at your Local Council. To find their Head Office, see www.tradingstandards.gov.uk, look at this page carefully, there is a box to enter your postcode and find the contact details for your area.[1]

Approved balances, classes of balance

First, the easy bit. A weighing machine used in trade must be stamped with a special sticker:

The 'M' is on a green background, the number (the 'office' number) is on a wavy blue-metallic background and should match the number of the certificate. This is the new European standard mark. The 'CE' is also a European standard mark, but (in this case) for electrical safety rather than 'use in trade'.

If you buy a new approved digital balance, make sure it comes with its certificate. This will be on the official paper of the Trading Standards office that approved it. It will be headed *Certificate of* Conformity or *Declaration of Conformity*, at the bottom will be the official seal, and the number on the certificate should match the number on the machine. If it is calibrated for use at a particular location, the name of the town will be printed after *The EC-verification is valid for the following installation/location area of use:* The body of the certificate will look like this:

---

[1] Alternatively, call your Local Council (at your local Council Offices or Town Hall) then ask for Trading Standards then ask for Weights & Measures (in a large Council this will be an entire department, in a small Council this will be one woman who works alternate Tuesdays).

The conformity of the non-automatic weighing instrument

Manufacturer:	
Type / Model:	
Serial number:	

with the requirements of the Council Directive 90/384/EEC as amended was established by tests referred to in EN 45 501 - 8.2.

The EC-verification is valid for the following place of installation/location/ area of use:

If you buy a secondhand digital balance, check that it has the approval marks and also a seal over the screws that open the balance (or the adjustment-screw that changes the calibration). This will either be a 'security sticker' marked *Do not Remove* or a lead seal and wire.

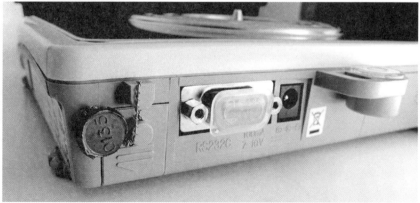

Old scales (eg. the old beam balance) can still be used for trade providing they have the Trading Standards crown as the approval mark, for more details, see page 61. The numbers are the office number and the year of testing (in this example it was approved in Derbyshire in 2007)

2007

1370

If a Weighs & Measures Inspector finds that the balance is not working correctly and cannot be used for trade, he cannot physically remove the balance (it's your property) but he will 'cancel' the approval mark by stamping a star over the top of the crown of 'M'.

There will also be a 'Class' number, eg. "Class II" or just "II"..

There are four Classes (grades) of approved balance:

CLASS 4
For heavy items such as Heavy Goods Vehicles

CLASS 3
For general goods, from light-ish (eg. herbs) to heavy-ish (bags of fruit)

CLASS 2
For items that have a high value per gram, specifically precious metals

CLASS 1
For scientific applications, eg. for weighing down to 0.001g

The above information is not generally known. For instance, my long-time supplier of approved balances had no idea about the different classes. Of two new suppliers one assured me, in writing, that Class 3 was OK for weighing precious metals (not true!) and the other simply said, 'It depends on where they are being used' (i.e. who is enforcing the law).

Now if you go into the intricate detail of the regulations you will find that the 2009 'guidelines' from the National Weights & Measures Laboratory to Weights & Measures Inspectors DO say that CLASS II must be used for weighing precious metals, but what I can't tell you is how this is enforced in your area. It might be that, having bought a CLASS III balance for £300.00, an inspector will insist that this just isn't good enough, and you need a CLASS II (from £500.00) or it might be that he will be so delighted you actually have an approved balance, he'll turn a blind eye to the 'detail' of the 'guidelines' and will move on to the thousands of traders who don't have an approved balance at all.

When you call your local Trading Standards, you need to get the 'feel' of how they enforce the law, I do not recommend helping them by quoting the 2009 guidelines from the National Weights & Measures Laboratory to Weights & Measures Authorities and asking if they agree!

Two Complications

- Complication No. 1: 1g or 0.1g or 0.01g?

The following concerns the more accurate CLASS II balances (for weighing precious metals).

When you buy an approved CLASS II balance (from about £500.00) the manufacturers will give you its specification, eg. that it weighs up to 150g in 0.05g steps, or that it weighs 2100g. in steps of 0.01g. What they WON'T tell you is that once it's approved, you are not supposed to use that last decimal place. So, for instance, having spent hundreds of pounds and thinking you will be weighing down to 0.1g you will discover that the balance now has a red cross painted over that last decimal place so that it only reads to the nearest 1g. (though the 0.1g will still be visible under the red cross).

This is OK in that you will only be advertising to buy (or sell) per gram. But when you actually do the calculation you will be weighing to the nearest 0.1g, So what happens if a Weights & Measures Inspector calls? On the one hand, he might take a dim view of you working to the letter of the law, weighing gold and calculating the value to the nearest 1g when it would be possible to calculate the value to the nearest 0.1g. On the other hand, he might object to you quoting prices to the nearest 0.1g when, according to the letter of the law, your balance should only be used to the nearest 1g. With 18ct gold over £10.00 per gram [2010], this matters!

There are two solutions. Either buy a *better* CLASS II balance (be prepared to spend close to £1000.00) that reads to 0.01g as a non-approved balance, downgraded to 0.1g when approved. Or buy the cheaper CLASS II balance (for use to the nearest 1g, as described above) and hope that the inspector has some common sense.

- Complication No. 2: balances calibrated by area

The cheaper Class III balances do not have to be especially calibrated (checked against actual weights), so there are no complications. But you might not be able to use them for weighing precious metals (see above).

The cheaper CLASS II balances are calibrated for a particular postcode. So if, for instance, you work from a location in Liverpool, then it will be calibrated for Liverpool. This means that if you work at fairs and markets all over the county you SHOULD have a weighing balance for each location. Again, how is this enforced by the inspectors? Is he likely to ask to see its Certificate to check that it's being used in the correct postcode area? In fact, I have never, ever, seen an approved balance used at any antiques fair or street market, so MAYBE the inspectors only visit shops dealing in large amounts of money rather than the relatively low-level trade at fairs and markets, MAYBE an inspector would be so amazed that you actually have an approved balance that he'll glance at the approval seal and immediately move on to the next trader.

Incidentally, you cannot recalibrate them, they are fixed (with the seal) to make sure you can't recalibrate them.

At this point, customers say to me, in exasperation, 'Just tell me which balance I need that is guaranteed 100% OK according to the law, and which I can carry around the country!'. The answer is to buy a more expensive (about £1000.00) balance. These are not calibrated for a particular area, they can be used anywhere. HOW this works is quite ingenious. You calibrate it by pressing a button, and then you can hear motors whirring as they lower an actual physical weight onto an internal weighing pan to reset the electronics to match the weight.

WEIGHING MACHINES

TWO METHODS OF WEIGHING

There are two methods of weighing based on two types of technology: comparing mass and measuring the effect of gravity. A 'mass' is the technical term for anything which is weighed, whether goods or weights.

Comparing Mass

Two pans (or hooks or scoops) rest either end of a beam (usually a strip of wood or metal). The beam is hung or pivoted in the middle so that the two pans balance. Goods are placed on one side and weights on the other. The weights are then varied until the two pans balance. Designs vary, on a jeweller's balance the pans hang down from the beam which is pivoted on a tall rod (pictured). On a greengrocer's balance the pans rest on top of the beam, which is hidden from sight. Both are beam balances.

The advantage of a beam balance is that it is very simple. Providing the pivots are not worn and the pointer points to zero the scale is in working order. Customers will notice if the two empty pans do not balance. The beam balance is easy for Weights & Measures Inspectors to check - they merely need to see that the pans 'balance' and that their test-weights balance with your weights.

Nobody makes approved beam balances any more, though you can find old models at antiques fairs. The approval stamp should be on the horizontal beam by the hinge. Check that each weight is stamped too.

The crown is the same Trading Standards mark found on glasses in pubs.

The middle number is the Office Number at which the item was tested.

The bottom number is the last two digits of the date, in this case 1989.

One warning about secondhand approved beam balances. I once found *the* most beautifully-engineered balance that folded out of a huge box and was an inspector's balance, used by Weights & Measures Inspectors. So I bought it, sold it to a shopkeeper, but first sent it to be re-stamped so that he knew it was still 'legal'. I then discovered that the approval mark, the portcullis and crown (illustrated below) was invalid. It was, the lady at Trading Standards told me, better than the equipment she used herself, but the portcullis-and-crown was the Board of Trade stamp, replaced in 1970, with the DTI (Department of Trade and Industry) crown. In other words, pre-1970 balances are not approved for use in trade and cannot be re-stamped.

Measuring the effect of gravity, spring balances and electronic balances

These do not require sets of weights as they do not compare mass. They measure the effect of gravity. This is good and bad. It is good that you don't have to go to the trouble of balancing weights against goods, but it is bad in that gravity varies from place to place.

The most popular portable balance is the spring balance. It is small (often pocket size) and fast to use. The disadvantage is that spring balances have a limited range: you may have to carry two or three, for light items, medium items and heavy items. Although it might be possible to design a spring balance capable of weighing light items (eg. in ½ gram steps) and heavy items (eg. up to 2000g), it would have to be a few feet long to contain all the graduations.

Spring balances designed for weighing suitcases do not have to be accurate - they weigh to the nearest 250g, are pocket size and cost under £5.00; spring balances used for gold and silver have large clear scales and sensitive long-lasting springs. The cheaper models cost around £10.00 and are made of plastic. The long brass models (usually by Salter) aren't made anymore but can sometimes be found at antiques markets and boot sales (check carefully that they are marked in Troy ounces for weighing silver and not Pounds and Ounces for fishing - see page 52). The best (Swiss-made) models cost about £50.00, are made of aluminium and are small enough to slip into the pocket.

Bathroom and kitchen scales, even if they are 'digital', are not accurate. At worst, they comprise a spring scale connected to an electronic circuit and are no more accurate than mechanical spring scales. A variation which produces slightly more realistic readings uses flat metal plates instead of springs, connected to an electronic circuit and a display - the 'electronic spring balance'. Typical prices: £15.00 to £30.00. Typical specifications: 2g increments up to 1000g or 5g increments up to 2000g or 10g increments up to 5000g or 200g increments up to 90kg. The lower-range models are useful for the quick appraisal of silver. One warning: do not switch these machines to ounces when weighing gold and silver, they weight in the Ounce Avoirdupois which is used for food and goods, not gold and silver.

Spring balances are still popular for weighing silver, but for weighing gold the digital (electronic) balance now reigns supreme.

Most electronic balances used for weighing gold and silver use a more sophisticated technology than simply connecting a spring to some electronics. The transducer[1] (the bit that does the measuring) can be quite sophisticated, and it is this that produces a good or bad electronic balance, all other features should be viewed as secondary. An analogy is that of a hi fi system - having lots of 'features' does not mean the system produces a good sound.

Prices of this type of electronic balance vary considerably depending upon the specification and general build quality. There are now many dozens of pocket-size models that sell for between £10.00 and £50.00, with larger table-top balances ranging from £30.00 to £60.00. Typically, these weigh in 0.01g increments up to 100g or 0.1g increments up to 500g or 1g increments up to 3000g. However, if you wish to keep the same resolution (eg. 0.1g) but with a high capacity (eg. 5000g) the price too will treble. The terms *resolution* and *capacity* (and *accuracy)* are explained below.

Some people get confused with decimal points, eg. 0.001g, 0.01g, 0.1g.

0.001g is for the accurate pricing of diamonds (typical resolution in carats, 0.01ct = 1pt) . The capacity of these balances is usually 10g or 20g.

---

[1] The weighing component comprises a strip of special metal with a hole drilled through it (a *load cell*). When the force of a weight is applied, the hole distorts. Sensors (strain gauges) across the hole measure the amount of distortion and produce an electrical signal, which is converted into units of weight on a display. This whole assembly is called a transducer.

0.01g. resolution is OK for weighing gemstones and diamonds approximately (typical resolution in carats is 0.05ct = 5 points), and is also good for powder for ammunition (weighed in grains, approx. 15 gr = 1g).

0.1g. resolution is best for gold and platinum, rare coins, model-aircraft parts, catalysts for adhesives, photographic chemicals. 0.1g of 9ct gold is worth about £8.00[1] (that's the actual gold value, you won't get this much selling scrap).

1g. resolution is fine for small silver items (1g of silver is worth about 38p) or for weighing letters and packets.

20g, 50g, or even 100g resolution is good for heavy silver, large parcels, suitcases etc. The capacity of these balances varies from 2.5Kg to 30Kg (80oz Troy to 950oz Troy). 1oz (31g) of silver is worth about £12.00. That's the actual silver value, you won't get this much selling scrap).

EVALUATING A WEIGHING MACHINE

Accuracy and Resolution

Accuracy is the true matching of a reading to a weight. If a balance reads '10g' when a 10g weight is weighed then it is accurate. Nothing is 100% accurate, there is always a degree of error, however small. Accuracy is expressed as a percentage. To find the error, multiply the percentage accuracy by the weight.[2] If a balance has an accuracy of 0.2% and you want to know the possible error on weighing 100g, calculate: 0.2% X 100g = 0.4g. In this example a 100g weight will measure 100g ± 0.4g. Accuracy suffers in extremes of temperature. A manufacturer may state a 'recommended operating temperature'. This point is worth noting if you are using the balance outside in the winter or if you wish to take the balance to a hot country.

The problem of accuracy does not apply on a beam balance because a beam balance does not measure weight, it compares mass. The accuracy of a beam balance depends purely on the accuracy of the weights used; and the accuracy of the weights can only be checked against another set of weights (usually that carried by the inspector of

---

[1] The prices on this page relate to 2010. Prices change dramatically over the months and years, so it's certain to be different by the time you read this.

[2] In Physics, at school, sentences like this used to drive me mad. I would say 'Multiply *what* weight?!'. The answer: multiply *any* weight. Simply think of a number of grams and pretend it's the weight of the item you are about to weigh.

weights and measures) who, in turn, checks his weights against a master set of weights back in the office...which are checked against a master set at Head Office...and so on to *the* master weight in Paris.

Resolution (otherwise known as readability) is the smallest unit of weight a weighing machine will measure. A balance which weighs down to 0.1g has a resolution of 0.1g. Resolution should not be confused with accuracy. If a weighing machine has a resolution of 0.1g and yet a 1g weight measures 1.8g the balance is not accurate but the resolution (readability) is still 0.1g.

Confusing accuracy with resolution can lead to disappointment. A kitchen balance with a resolution of 1g and a capacity of 2000g may have an accuracy of 2.0%. This means that if you commonly weigh items of 1500g the reading on the display will only be accurate to within ± 30g. (i.e. 2.0% X 1500g = 30g), not too bad if weighing flour but useless if weighing gold. An inexpensive balance of the same resolution, designed for jewellery, may have an accuracy of 0.2%, bringing the possible error on weighing 1500g down to 3g. This error may not bother you, but if it does you should aim for a balance with an accuracy of 0.02%, thus reducing the possible error on 1500g to under 1g. A kitchen version of this balance may cost £20.00, a cheap jewellery version £50.00 and a good jewellery version over £200.00.

Capacity

Capacity is the maximum weight a weighing machine will measure. Some weighing machines will weigh more than the recommended maximum but may then give inaccurate readings.

Sensitivity

An over sensitive beam balance will swing one way and the other and never settle in the middle, eg. if using a sensitive glass-cased laboratory balance for weighing gold. An under sensitive beam balance will remain balanced even when weights are placed on one side, eg. decorative folding balances from India. An over sensitive spring balance will bob up and down and not settle, an under sensitive spring balance will not move at all. In practice, sensitivity is only a problem when weighing objects which are too light or too heavy for the balance.

Repeatability

A beam balance will always give the same reading: if you place the same weight on each side, it will balance - every time. Other types of weighing balance do not always give the same reading. The springs of spring balances and the load cells of electronic balances stretch with time and are also sensitive to extremes of temperature. Spring balances have an adjustable zero, electronic balances are built so that they self-zero (auto-tare) each time a button is pressed.

Extra features on electronic balances

The capacity and accuracy of an electronic balance depends upon the quality of the transducer. All other 'features' are due to the sophistication of the electronics.

Mains or battery. Some balances are expensive to run on batteries, others are so cheap to run on batteries that it is not worth buying a mains transformer; some take standard AA or AAA batteries, some of the smaller balances take button batteries. Approved balances tend to be mains-only, though there are Class III versions designed for the catering trade that are battery-operated and waterproof (they can be washed in a sink) - but these are not usually permitted for buying and selling gold and silver. Class II versions are always advertised as mains-only, but if you ask, *sometimes* battery packs (at about £200.00) are available to special order. For an explanation of *Class III* and *Class II* see page 56.

Tare. The scale will read zero each time a button is pressed, even if goods are already on the weighing platform, so that you can place a tray or dish on the platform, tare it, then pour the items on. This is standard on all balances these days.

Low battery indicator. Important since electronic balances will work on low batteries but may give inaccurate readings.

Calibration facility. Checks the accuracy by the placing of a weight on the pan and setting the display to that weight[1].

Multi-unit. Weighs in more than one unit, eg. grams or ounces or pennyweight or grains, each at the flick of a switch. This is useful if you

---

[1] In practice, the cheaper the balance the more complicated the procedure. You will need to buy a calibration weight. With very cheap balances, you must press several buttons in a strict sequence otherwise you 're-program' the computer in the balance and have to send it back to the supplier. Expensive balances require just one press of a button. The cheaper *Class II* balances cannot be calibrated, they are 'fixed' so that they can't be tampered with. Expensive *Class II* balances have the calibration weight hidden inside the machine, when you press the button you can actually hear a motor placing a physical weight onto an internal sensor. For more details see page 160.

actually use these various systems of weights on a regular basis, alternatively, consider buying an electronic calculator for £5.00 rather than spending an extra £50.00 for the facility.

Other features:

Auto-tare. It can be set to assume that the first item placed on the weighing platform is a container, so it stays on zero, then automatically weighs whatever you pour into the container (all balances have this function but you have to press a button: manual tare).

Environmental adjustment. It can be set to ensure accurate readings in stable conditions (eg. a calm shop at room temperature) or unstable (eg. with vibrations and changes of temperature).

Parts counting. Place some samples on the platform and press some buttons. Now instead of weighing it will 'count' the number of components you place on the platform.

Percentage measuring. Place your sample on the platform and press some buttons. Now each item will display as a percentage of the sample.

Connect to printer or computer. This will give you the option of controlling the balance from a computer. My advice: do not play with this function unless you are a computer expert.

Hanging-weight facility. Instead of placing items on the platform, you can hang them from underneath. Place the entire balance on a specially-designed frame (an expensive accessory), weigh the item, then dangle the item in a container of water and weigh it again. The balance will calculate the item's specific gravity.

Internal calibration system. There are some actual physical weights inside the scale. If it hasn't been used for more than a few hours or the temperature changes by more than 1.5 degrees, you must calibrate it. This is easy, you press two buttons and you hear the motors inside as it tests the electronics against the weights.

Finally, there are features on some advanced balances that I really don't understand: Tael, Tical, Momme, Mesghal, factor, multiplier and LSD (that means Least Significant Digit not Lysergic acid diethylamide). On the basis that you are weighing gold and silver and not working in a physics laboratory, I suggest ignoring these.

VALUATIONS

A jewellery valuer[1] should have a mixture of hands-on experience in the jewellery trade and qualifications resulting from extensive study, kept up to date by reading periodicals and by attending conferences, training courses and trade shows. The main qualifications are FGA, PJ Gem Dip and PJ Val Dip, which are currently the only specialist British qualification for jewellery valuers, but there are others[2].

Professional jewellery valuing has moved on spectacularly in the last few years. Gone are the days of the quickly written one-liner, 'Three Stone Diamond Ring, £1000.' Nowadays, the written valuation certificate should comprise an 'appraisal', a detailed description of the item, and a 'valuation' should be accompanied by 'notes to the valuation', an explanation of terminologies and the basis of valuations. It might also include photographs. The valuer will also keep any 'working notes' for his files, should any future questions arise or the need for an updated valuation. It is quite normal for a professional valuer to spend an hour over a single item.

You do have to pay for all this work and not all valuers charge in the same way. As an hourly charge, £40.00 is quite reasonable; as a flat rate, between £20.00 and £35.00 for the first item, with a discount for subsequent items (£10.00 to £15.00 each if there are many); as a percentage, anywhere from ½% to 2½%. There might also be a small percentage surcharge for high-value items. Prices will be higher when a shop takes in goods for valuation, then sends them to the valuer - they want to make a profit. V.A.T. may be chargeable.

VALUATION FOR INSURANCE

A valuation for insurance states the amount of money an insurance company would pay if the item had to be replaced as new at some time in the future. If this sounds a little vague, it is. Insurance valuations can never be exact, it depends on the current value of gold and gemstones, gemstone treatments, fashion, politics (eg. reduced supply of gems from

---

[1] My thanks to valuer Gail Hislop PJ Gem Dip, PJ Val Dip, FNAG, MIRV for most of the information and some of the text in this section.

[2] Look for the letters MIRV (or FIRV), Member (or Fellow) of the Institute of Registered Valuers (formerly The National Association of Goldsmiths [NAG] Registered Valuers); or GVJ, (Guild of Valuers & Jewellers); or AJV, The Association Of Jewellery Valuers. For gemstones: FGA, (Fellow of the Gemmological Association); PJ GEM DIP (Professional Jewellers Gemmological Diploma); or the specialist qualification in diamonds, DGA (Diamond Member of the Gemmological Association).

a war-torn country), brand name, history, quality of workmanship, desirability, condition, rarity etc. Oral valuations for insurance purposes should not be relied upon, in fact they are expressly forbidden by some trade associations, though this does not prevent the *non*-professional valuer (including jewellery salesmen, scrap merchants and antiques traders) offering advice.

VALUATION FOR PROBATE

Probate values (used for the calculation of Inheritance Tax) are required by Her Majesty's Revenue and Customs (HMRC) to reflect the going value of an item in a free market. Whereas it was once standard to think of a 'lowest possible value' that any trader, anywhere, would eagerly offer, nowadays it's more common to use auction prices. A valuer will understand that the value has to be low, but will also be aware that Revenue & Customs might later ask what price you got when you sold the goods, compared with the probate valuation.

VALUATION FOR AUCTION

An auction valuation is really an estimate as to how much an item might fetch at auction. You could be lucky and get more, you could be could be unlucky and get less - it depends purely on who is bidding. Estimates are often embarrassingly inaccurate, as publicised by the press each time bidders enter into a 'bidding war' and bid several times the estimate. It also often happens that an item is, theoretically, extremely rare and valuable but attracts virtually no interest and the highest bid is way below the reserve price.

THE 'PUB VALUATION' AND VALUATION TO SELL

When shopping around for the best price to sell gold and silver you will find that each person in the jewellery trade has a speciality. Most people know something about everything, yet the diamond merchant may know little about coins, the numismatist little about pearls, the antiques trader little about bullion. Worst of all is the friend in the pub who claims that your gold ring is worth £100.00 when he doesn't know anything at all.

There is no such thing as a valuation that states how much an item can be sold for. If that ring - the one valued at £100.00 in the pub - can be sold for £200.00 then its selling value is £200.00. If everyone agrees that it must be worth *at least* £100.00 but the most anyone is willing to pay is £50.00 then its selling value is £50.00. I call these wildly misleading valuations 'pub valuations' because it usually emerges that the friend in the pub had consumed eight pints of beer before suddenly realising he was an expert in valuing gold and silver.

Just as worthless is the 'selling valuation' given by someone who quotes a buying price but then says he is not actually buying anything at the moment.

CLEANING AND POLISHING

Gold does not change colour although 9ct gold dulls due to the copper and silver in the alloy. Silver turns black (tarnishes) when exposed to the air. Copper (and copper-based alloys) dull to a deep brown over the years.

The stones in jewellery often appear dull because soap and gunge build up behind the setting. The best treatment is to rub a paste cleaner (eg. a 'non-scratch bath cleaner') into the setting then give a brisk brush with an old toothbrush and plenty of hot water. If you do this under a running tap, ensure that there is a plug in the sink just in case a stone falls out - any jeweller can re-set a stone, not so many can replace them. Commercial jewellery cleaners are available from jewellery shops, hardware shops and department stores, either in paste or liquid form. Finally, shine the gold with a soft cloth.

A tip for polishing gold rings: smear some jeweller's polishing rouge (stick form is more easily handled than powder) onto several strands of linen thread. Pull the multi-stranded thread taught (tie one end to a heavy object or get a friend to help). Now rub the ring vigorously up and down the thread. In this way, the outside *and* inside of the ring can be polished with ease.

Silver goes black (tarnishes) due to sulphur in the air[1]. Many substances cause silver to tarnish. PVC (polyvinyl chloride) so don't wrap silver in plastic bags, gas from cooking (from the sulphur in coal gas, not from natural gas), cigarette smoke, rubber (don't fix silver cutlery together with elastic bands), even sunlight.

Silver cleaners are messy and smelly so wear gloves. If the smell gives you a headache work outside in the fresh air. A silver dip solution will

---

[1] The reaction is *not* oxidisation (the reaction that produces rust in iron).

remove tarnish. It can be found in small jars (the lid may stick: lubricate it with a candle) or in five litre canisters (sold to the catering trade). Make a wire holder and hang the silver items in the solution. Don't forget to remove the items after a few minutes. I once left a fine silver chain in silver dip for two weeks. It dissolved.

Impregnated 'long term' silver polishing cloths (also available as 'polishing mittens') or wadding will clean large flat areas more easily than silver dip and also slow down the rate of tarnish. There are impregnated wadding cleaners designed for copper and steel too.

After cleaning and polishing, silver can be protected from tarnish by spraying with lacquer. The most effective (and most expensive) method of preventing tarnishing altogether is to plate the item with another metal such as rhodium or palladium. However, it is simpler to clean items in silver dip then use a 'long term' wadding or foam silver cleaner. It should not need cleaning again for a few months.

There is an easy way of removing tarnish from silver without resort to messy cleaners (though the item will still need polishing afterwards).

Find a container large enough to completely immerse the items in water. The container must not be made of metal (use a glass, enamel[1] or plastic bowl). Place in the container some crumpled aluminium foil, salt and sodium bicarbonate. The quantities aren't critical, approx. a quarter of a cup of sodium bicarbonate and a teaspoon of salt per litre will do. Add boiling water and stir. Now place the items in the container and watch the tarnish vanish.

The items must touch each other and must touch the aluminium foil. If you use a disposable aluminium container you don't need the aluminium foil. You can use a container made of another metal (eg. steel or copper) providing you very carefully line it with the aluminium foil so that none of the silver touches the metal of the container. However, it easier to use a non-metal container and it is more effective to crumple the aluminium foil.

Some people hear the word 'soda' and use the wrong chemical. You must use sodium bicarbonate, $NaHCO_3$ (also known as bicarbonate of soda, sodium bicarb or baking powder). If you use sodium carbonate, CNa_2O_3 (also known as Soda, Washing Soda or Soda Ash) it won't work.

You may have seen, at antiques or craft fairs, stands selling a 'magic'

---

[1] The enamel must not be chipped

metal plate and a 'chemical' - the metal plate is a piece of aluminium and the chemical is salt and sodium bicarbonate. If you are a silver dealer who has to clean large quantities of silver, there's no harm in buying one of these plates rather than having to use huge amounts of aluminium foil.

Do not clean or polish coins as it completely destroys their collector's value. Medals often become polished merely through wearing and this cannot be avoided. A coin which has been buried in the ground may be washed gently with water to clean away surface dirt. Coin dealers use solvents to clean coins which are so dirty (or mouldy) that they are otherwise unsaleable, a risky operation which can destroy the coin's value completely. Mould occasionally grows on gold coins, often on copper coins, it spreads and is nearly impossible to remove, so keep them away from good coins. Remove sticky marks (eg. from sticky tape) with acetone or petrol. Coins of no value at all (most pre-decimal copper and brass coins) are best cleaned with a 'metal cleaner' such as copper or brass polish or, for ingrained dirt, soaked in a salt and vinegar solution overnight. Scrubbing with HP sauce has a similar effect but is very messy. Coin jewellery becomes polished with wear and will not be further damaged by polishing.

To remove every scratch requires professional polishing. All jewellery repairers carry out this service though few advertise it. Ask your jeweller to 'polish as new'. The cost shouldn't be more than £5.00 or £10.00 and the result is an item as clean and bright as the day it was made. Jewellery repairers polish *every* item they repair. If you send antique jewellery for repair and do *not* want it 'polished as new' give the clear instruction 'clean only, do not polish.' The items will then be cleaned brightly (this must be done, as gold and silver emerge black after soldering) but not polished to a mirror finish.

PART TWO: BUYING AND SELLING

BUYING AND SELLING

SELLING

BUYING

BUYING AND SELLING FOR PROFIT

BUYING AND SELLING BULLION, 127

TAX, 129

FUTURES TRADING, GOLD LEASING, 131

BUYING AND SELLING

PAPER MONEY AND GOLD MONEY

Once gold was the currency of the world, the bartering medium of the world's economy. Each UK currency note contains a promise *I PROMISE TO PAY THE BEARER ON DEMAND THE SUM OF [value of the note]* and is signed *FOR THE GOVERNOR AND COMPANY OF THE BANK OF ENGLAND [signature] CHIEF CASHIER.* This promise was once true: you could take a pound note into a bank and change it for a pound's worth of gold (a gold sovereign). The notes were merely promissory notes for looking after your gold. If you wanted the gold back, any bank would hand it back over the counter in exchange for the notes.[1] if you did not want to carry gold coins, you could exchange them for notes in any bank.

This system of paper-money-for-gold-money was world-wide and was known as the gold standard. In the aftermath of the First World War, the system slowly began to collapse and by the 1920s governments were printing paper money which was not supported by gold - you could no longer insist on gold in exchange for notes. It was soon noticed that the gold sovereign could be sold for a few pennies more than face value. Gradually the gold price rose and today a gold sovereign costs nearly two hundred pounds of paper money[2].

WHAT HAPPENS WHEN GOVERNMENTS BUY AND SELL GOLD

Governments still keep their 'spare cash' in the form of gold - it is called the Gold Reserve. In Britain this is kept in the vaults of The Bank of England; in the United States it is kept in Fort Knox. A government might release some of its gold reserve so that it can raise money to pay back loans to other governments or to finance a war. Often, these events are kept secret,[3] a government does not want it known that its economy is weak and it urgently needs extra cash.

---

[1] I have a long letter from a customer elaborating on this statement, saying that it was sovereigns (gold £1.00 coins) that could be changed for gold bars, and quoting various sources, see page 159 for a summary of his letter.

[2] This amount will vary hugely from month to month and year to year, so this figure is likely to be completely inaccurate by the time you read this.

[3] Sometimes it is not so secret, for instance Prime Minister Gordon Brown sold half the country's gold reserves between 1999 and 2002 (395 Tonnes) and the press are keen to point out that if he had waited until 2010 he would have got three times more money...but nobody knew that at the time.

The result of a sudden influx of gold onto the world market is to lower the price of gold. It was long-suspected that a powerful government could also arrange for the world price of gold to rise. This is probably what happened in 1979 when the Iranians took American diplomats hostage. The price of gold rose dramatically, much to the bewilderment of the entire world. Then, in 1980, the United States government conceded that a ransom would have to be paid. Since paper money was quite out of the question (what would the Iranians do with millions of dollar bills?) the only alternatives were arms or gold. The Americans refused to pay a ransom in arms and so a weight of gold was arranged. As soon as the ransom had been paid the price of gold mysteriously fell as dramatically as it had risen - the Iranian's gold was now worth far less than when the amount was negotiated. This is just an example of how political (in addition to economic) factors affect the price of gold, for a more detailed analysis, see page 45.

WHAT HAPPENS WHEN YOU BUY OR SELL GOLD

The pages which follow are full of hints and tips about buying and selling. Most useful of these is the list of rates you should expect when selling scrap and bullion. To an extent, 'standard rates' for scrap are academic. If someone quotes a buying price for a small 9ct ring, it's just a price for the seller and buyer to agree, there isn't *necessarily* a fixed 'rate'.

For saleable items (definitely not scrap...though that can be a matter of opinion) the price can be even more variable. The buyer may have a customer eager to buy your item and so can offer a high price, or he may be overdrawn at the bank that day and only want to pay a low price. Providing you are not in a hurry, you can hold out for the best price, whether buying or selling, and happily ignore the advice which follows.

THE THREE PRICES OF GOLD AND SILVER

There are three prices of gold and silver. The official price, the selling price and the buying price.

If you are a trader then, hopefully, you will buy at the lower price and sell at the higher price. The official price of the moment (the 'spot price' or 'actual gold value') can be found from a number of sources (see page 43) and forms a *guide* to buying and selling. Traders may, in practice, charge or ask any amount they wish. Only in the bullion and scrap trade are there standard buying and selling prices relative to the actual gold value, see the section on Buying and Selling Bullion on page 127.

SELLING

WHERE TO SELL AND HOW MUCH TO EXPECT

The price of gold changes each day. For details of how the prices are fixed, see page 43; for details of how to calculate the actual gold value of an item see page 47; for details of where to find the latest gold price, see page 45.

It is tempting to think that, because an item cost a great amount of hard work and was given with great love and treasured for many years, its value in money is great. This is not so. If you are selling an item because it is broken or showing signs of wear or out of fashion then it *will* be worth only scrap value. A pretty but lightweight chain may have cost £50.00 or £60.00 to buy new but comprise only £10.00 or £15.00 of gold. Out-of-fashion dress rings with small stones, even if they are diamonds, are similarly priced. Silver is worth even less. A silver neck chain may have cost £10.00 but its resale value will be only a few pence. Coins or medallions are often listed in catalogues and brochures as *collectable* but if demand is limited only scrap value will be realised, there will *be* no 'historic' or 'artistic' value, even after several years, you *will* have to settle for just a tiny fraction of its original price[1]. But look on the bright side: gold and silver have a high scrap value compared to most items - you wouldn't buy a new car then expect to recover most of your money on scrap steel.

Scrap value (melt value) is not the same as 'official' gold value (actual gold value): scrap value is lower. This is because smelters charge a percentage of the gold value for their service and scrap dealers sell to the smelters and must make a profit (and your local jeweller probably sells to the scrap dealer and must make a profit). In the case of the nationally-advertised *Buy Your Gold!* companies, they are paying many millions of pounds on newspaper and television advertising, and must recover their money by offering very low rates.

The advantage of taking gold directly to smelters is that the highest rates are paid. The disadvantage is that they will buy only in quantity. Smelters also levy a standard charge (between £50.00 and £100.00) for the melt and assay of non-hallmarked items which must be paid even if the metal proves to be worthless.

---

[1] By the time the jewellery has reached a shop, its selling price is around five times the value of the gold - that was the general 'formula' I used in the 1980s, the same proportion was found in a 2009 survey by the Consumer Association, the same proportion was quoted by a professional jewellery valuer in 2010.

Most people do not have access to a smelter and so will go to the nearest jewellers shop advertising to buy gold and silver, or send their gold to any one of a dozen nationally-advertised gold-buying companies who will buy any quantity no matter how small. Rates tend to be higher when the price of gold is stable, when it fluctuates wildly jewellers operating on narrow margins must offer a lower percentage or risk losing money if the price falls.

JEWELLERS AND SCRAP DEALERS IN PERSON

Selling to jewellers (whether in a high street shop or market stall) can be good or bad. If they appear puzzled then search through piles of old newspapers before offering a price, then they may not be up-to-date. If they make a telephone call or look on the internet then the chances are that they are up to date. It is advisable, when shopping around for the best price, to compare rates on the same day. It is also possible (not *very* likely...but possible) that the jeweller will like the look of your item and offer more than scrap value because he can sell it as an item in the window - that is something the *Buy Your Gold!* mail order companies will not do.

Everybody will advertise BEST PRICES PAID - this means that they will offer the price they think best. Anyone specialising in scrap will work on a percentage of the gold price (even if they won't tell you what that percentage is) so do your best to find out that percentage. But don't become obsessed - if your sale is a one-off, getting a 5% better price relative to the 'spot' (actual / official) price is irrelevant when that 'spot' price can be 15% higher or 15% lower next week or next month.

Also bear in mind that you have more negotiating power when dealing with large amounts of money. If the approximate gold value of your coins is £5000.00 it's worth hunting around for that extra 1%. If the approximate gold value of your earring is £12.00, a jeweller might offer you only £7.00 on the basis that he doesn't regard any transaction worthwhile for less than £5.00 profit, so offering £7.00 is (in his opinion) doing you a big favour. But look on the bright side: if you are stranded and the only way to raise money for the bus fare home is to sell a gold earring, think yourself lucky that you have something of value that is instantly saleable.

THE ALL-PURPOSE HIGH STREET SECONDHAND / LOANS SHOPS

These shops don't actually have a generic name. They offer cheque-cashing services, changing pay-cheques for cash or giving an advance on your salary, changing any cheque for cash,[1] changing cash or cheques for foreign currency, instant cash loans, logbook loans,[2] and pawnbroking.[3] Typical are The Money Shop (over 250 shops in the U.K, see www.moneyshop.tv) and Cheque Centre (over 140 shops, see www.chequecentre.co.uk). Two other chains have diversified. Their services now include buy-backs,[4] Western Union money transfers, and buying scrap gold and silver (in fact, they now buy nearly anything[5]). And if none of that suits your needs, howabout the free debt advice service? See Cash Converters (www.cashconverters.co.uk, over 170 shops) and Cash Generator (www.cashgenerator.co.uk, over 100 shops).

Having found themselves with shops full of 'things' to sell, they have expanded by selling them on the internet (the shop posts the goods) or to callers (order online, collect from the shop).

SCRAP BY MAIL / FROM THE INTERNET

On the good side, the internet provides a huge choice of companies willing to buy your gold, and you can spend many hours admiring their websites. On the bad side, if you telephone you will usually get through to a Call Centre where the answer to all but the simplest questions will be, 'I don't know, we just send out the packs' (a prepaid envelope).

In 2010 we telephoned five nationally-advertised companies. Here are some of the things to look out for:

- Is there a calculator on the website (you enter the weight and carat and get a price) or are you expected to send the goods without having any idea of the value? Of the seven nationally-advertised websites we examined, only one had a calculator. None would

---

[1] An advertisement on the radio added, "...providing we are happy with the cheque and with your identification"

[2] A loan against a car...though you get to keep the car unless you default on the loan.

[3] Lending money against valuables, usually gold.

[4] Unlike pawnbroking, 'title' (ownership) stays with the original owner for one month, after which it passes to the shop, unless the customer buys it back (the shop, of course, makes a small profit).

[5] Just about the only things they don't buy are weapons (including anything sharp) and clothing.

confirm a price, and when we said we had 2g of 9ct gold, six out of the seven had no idea how much that might be worth.

- Do they automatically buy the gold or do they make an offer and wait for you to accept or decline? On the telephone they all said they make an offer, one said that if they don't hear from you in 12 days they send the item back. However, one had written terms stating that you must ask for a quote, otherwise they will *automatically* buy it (and melt it).

- Is the postage *to* them pre-paid? All said they send out prepaid envelopes (maximum insurance for lost in transit, £500.00). But please think about this - the envelopes cost money and that money has to be recovered, so you might be better off paying the postage and using a no-frills company that pays a higher rate.

- Is the postage back to you free (if you decide not to sell)? All said there was no charge for the return of items if you decide not to sell. But upon reading the small print we found one company with a £10.00 charge for returning the goods if it turned out that *none* of the items were gold or silver.

- How do they pay? All offered payment by cheque, three also offered the option of transferring money directly into a bank account, one also offered cash (but they charge for the last two services).

- How long do they take to pay? This varied from one working day to 'about ten days', though two companies refused to give a time, saying that it depended on how quickly you accepted their offer.

We also asked, 'Just out of interest...' how they tested the gold. The answers were interesting:

- We just send it off and it's tested
- We use a magnet
- We get a jeweller to test it
- We test it here but I don't know how
- We use a magnet then an x-ray gun
- We take it to a jeweller, I think he uses a chemical
- We use acid

All of the above were the nationally-advertised companies that appeared during the 2010 gold boom, many of which ran newspaper and television advertising campaigns...and most of which will evaporate the moment the gold price crashes - and that is why I have not named them. Newspaper and television advertising campaigns are expensive, which is why these companies offer very low rates.

TRADE BUYERS OF SCRAP AND BULLION

An option for the trade (bulk) seller is to post the gold to (or visit the trade counters of) a long-established bullion dealer / scrap merchant. Please do check before sending small amounts of gold, rates will not be as high as their advertised 'trade' rates, or they may not accept small amounts at all. Here is a selection from around the country:

Michael Bloomstein (Brighton)
01273 608374. info@bloomsteins.co.uk
Small family-run business. In the tradition of trade bullion dealers payment is by return of post, also melt and assay service.

Cookson Precious Metals
0845 100 1122 or 0121 200 2120.
www.cooksongold.com/scrapgold/ birmingham.sales@cooksongold.com
Very large US-based company best known for providing precious metals for manufacturing jewellery.

Baird & Co.
London (E6) 0207 474 1000, London (EC1) 0207 831 2838
Glasgow 0141 248 5646.
sales@goldline.co.uk
Specialists in bullion coins. In-house refining of scrap.

Stephen Betts Group
Birmingham 0121 2332413
www.bettsmetals.com/ sbs@bettsmetals.co.uk
Refiners

Engelhard Refiners, part of BASF
This is a massive international company, so carefully find your way to www.catalysts.basf.com/Main/precious_base_metal_services/refining.be
Cinderford, Gloucestershire, 01594 827 744
Although they refine precious metal in any form, they specialise in reclaiming gold and platinum from electrical equipment and catalytic converters.

eBay (online auction)

eBay is an internet auction. You advertise ('list') your goods, buyers place bids, the highest bidder usually gets round to paying, you also get to pay eBay and PayPal lots of money for using the service.

Each item *will* take between 45 minutes and an hour to create (at first, allow two hours per item, eBay is complicated, learning is slow). So if you have little experience (or little patience) with computers, this is not for you.

However, as a hobby, and if you forget the fact that eBay is about the most complicated computer-based system in existence, and that you will spend hundreds of hours on the computer and will sometimes make a profit and sometimes make a loss – then go for it!

In the knowledge that most items are worth only scrap price, remember to list the carat and weight. For obviously-more-than-scrap items such as large diamond rings and antique items in nice condition eBay can sometimes work. I found that 'generic' items that are difficult to describe (unless you are a diamond expert, you will not be able to grade a diamond accurately) attract few buyers. For rare antique items, for which you might find more collectors in other parts of the world than in your home town, eBay can be useful. But it's an auction, it's a gamble, you can spend a huge amount of time listing items and not sell anything at all, or you can get more than you had expected.

There is a more detailed analysis of eBay in the section *Buying and Selling for Profit* on page 119.

THE INTERNET: SELLING FROM A WEBSITE

It is not difficult to create a simple website containing a handful of pages. There are many computer programs that make it simple, usually with 'templates' so that you follow a series of instructions and end up with a fixed design. Many ISPs (Internet Service Providers) are keen to sell you space on their servers for websites. They will provide or recommend programs.

For advanced website design have a look at *Dreamweaver.* It is very 'sophisticated' (there are even part time college courses teaching it) but it does have the advantage of working on different levels: the beginner can design pages as if on a word processor, advanced users can work entirely in htm (computer code).

You will need to take digital photos and insert them into the website. The problem with photo-enhancement programs is not where to find them, but which to choose. There will be at least two that come free with your computer (even *Paint* will do, if you have nothing else) and every camera comes with its free software. If you already have your favourite and all you want to do is to crop and resize photographs, and change the brightness, contrast, sharpness and colour balance – then stick with what you've got. If you want to paste out unwanted people or design catalogue covers, then go for something better. The software that professionals use is *Photoshop.[1]* The full version is very expensive but there are many 'downgraded' versions, some of which come free with other software.

If you like to get everything for free, search for free software (search for *freeware* or *shareware* or o*pen source).* These are computer programs written by enthusiasts, they are free, many are very good, but there is no support, if you have a problem you will have to search internet forums for the solution.

Take care when writing the text as vague descriptions will confuse readers. For instance, *heavy gold bracelet with white stones* is bad whereas *9ct gold bracelet with six white sapphires, weight 21g.* is better.

Websites get near the top of a Google search mostly by being popular. They have to get many of thousands of hits[2] and this *will* take months or years. You need to advertise your website in any way you can, from your visiting cards and headed paper, to newspaper adverts and brochures.

If selling from a website is more than a hobby, you will need to make sure it is e-commerce-enabled. That means it has a 'shopping basket', customers can click *Buy Now* and be forwarded to a payment system that accepts credit cards, see page 122123 for details.

KNOCKERS, TRAVELLERS, ROADSHOWS

Door-to-door buyers (known as, 'knockers') will offer to buy anything of value, including gold. Often they leaflet an area in advance, telling you who they are and explaining that they are really very honest. Personally, I don't see that a leaflet with a mobile phone number proves anything, but you don't *have* sell to knockers. It's up to you.

---

[1] Photoshop is by the company Adobe. They now call their *suite* of programs *CS* (*Creative Suite*) which includes Photoshop.

[2] A 'hit' is registered each time a page, photograph or link is viewed. This can be ten times the number of 'unique visitors' since each visitor will register as several *hits*.

Please do follow your usual precautions regarding letting strangers into your home, eg. by having the goods ready to show them at the door and never leaving strangers unattended while you go away to look for things or make a cup of tea.[1]

A variation on a theme is for the buyer to leaflet houses and place adverts in local newspapers, saying that he will be in town for one day only. He will then rent a room or small hall in a hotel (he might even call it a 'roadshow' with 'free valuations') - *you* visit *him* with your valuables.

I do not recommend these as methods of selling *unless* you have already done your research and are confident that the price is good, in which case - why not?

SILVER

It can be difficult to find good rates for small quantities of silver. This is because most jewellers buy silver in such small quantities that it can be months until they have enough to send to the smelters and they must allow for the possibility of the silver price falling over these months.

Unlike gold, a price per ounce is often quoted for *antique* items, though, of course, the price is much higher than scrap value....usually. The problem is that when the price of silver is very high, the scrap value exceeds the collector's value. Then, as the price of silver falls, collectors can once more afford to spend more than scrap value.

This extraordinary phenomenon has had strange repercussions. During the gold and silver boom of 1979-1980 (and also in the current gold boom) countless antiques were melted as their scrap value soared to many times that of any possible aesthetic value. It was in 1980 that we bought a Victorian ice bucket. The value of the silver was over £1000.00. The value to a collector was £200.00 or £300.00. We melted it. An art historian, who happened to be in the shop at the time, raised his hands in disbelief, how could such art treasures be melted? Antique silver dealers raised their hands in disbelief too - how can they make a living if prices are so high that even wealthy collectors could not afford to buy? This situation has arisen at various times throughout history.

---

[1] But common sense please, a single woman in a city centre flat faced by two large men will take more precautions than two men in a cottage on a Scottish island.

A WORD ABOUT STYLE

You walk into a jewellers shop with an item for sale. The shopkeeper may ask how much you want for it. His reasoning is as follows: if he puts an item in his window he does not ask his customers how much they would like to pay, he *tells* them how much he wants, and so if you are the one selling an item *you* should state the price. This is the style I grew up with in my grandfather's jewellers shop.

If you have some idea as to what price to expect (based, maybe, on a percentage of the original purchase price) then tell the jeweller, but don't calculate the price by starting with a price you have seen in a shop window and then doubling it - if your asking price is many times that which the jeweller can pay then he will prefer to say he is not interested rather than insult you with a low offer.

This is not the style of all buyers. Many assume that you are going from shop to shop for the best price and will simply make an offer. This is the style we used at the jewellers / bullion dealers where I worked for six years. I would test the gold, weigh it, calculate the price, and never know if my offer would shock or delight the seller.

If you receive what seems to be an unbelievably low offer keep calm, smile and say 'Thank you. I'll think about it'. This response is better than saying 'YOU MUST BE JOKING!!!' since the offer *may* be the highest you will receive and you may wish to return to that shop.

If several traders offer you a price which varies, for instance, from £50.00 to £70.00 then the market price *is* somewhere between £50.00 and £70.00, there is no conspiracy to offer you a low price. The traders are in competition for your custom. If you think it's worth more, your choices are: wait and hope the price of gold goes up, take a chance and put it into auction (you could get a lot more or a lot less), or sell it privately.

So what prices are to be expected? Usually scrap value, but by no means always, many items are worth more. The following is a rough guide as to how much to expect. I must stress that this guide is approximate.

SCRAP VALUES

For very large quantities (or from a bulk trade buyer): between 95% and 97% of actual gold value. Rates tend to be high when the prices are stable (or going up steadily) but *will* be lower when prices are depressed. Unless you are a very serious trade seller you will not get these rates!

For reasonably large quantities of gold (or from any 'keen' buyer): between 85% and 95% of actual gold value. If you get these rates for small amounts of gold you are doing really well.

For small quantities of gold: between 70% and 85% of actual gold value. These are good average rates. If you get a few percent more you are doing well, if you get a few percent less, not so well, but overall you should be pleased.

For tiny quantities of gold: between 50% and 70% of actual gold value.

For any quantity from the nationally-advertised *Sell Your Gold* mail order companies: the highest rate we got was 23% and the lowest was 8%. See page 173 for an analysis of my survey.

Getting only half of the actual gold value isn't very good but you might decide that for a tiny amount of gold and an easy sale it will do. I recommend that you do not accept less than half. In my opinion this is the point at which a very low price becomes unacceptably low.

These rates are *very* approximate. A large bullion dealer may decide to offer low rates for small quantities or the same rate for everyone. A local jeweller may offer the lowest rate of all (maybe he doesn't really understand scrap) or the highest rate of all (maybe he encourages the customers to use the money to buy jewellery from him).

These percentages are of the actual gold value, a figure that can be precisely calculated (see page 43) *not* a percentage of the retail price as a new (or antique) item.

Sometimes the value of the gold far exceeds any possible resale value as an item of jewellery, sometimes the antique or gemstone value is many times that of the gold value. However, most items of modern jewellery that have no gemstone, antique or collectable value *are* only worth scrap.

IF THE ITEM IS WORTH MORE THAN SCRAP

If the item is heavy the scrap price may far-exceed any possible resale value as an item of jewellery, no matter where it is sold, so start by calculating the scrap price. If you find that the scrap value really is nominal, and you are convinced that it's saleable as an item of jewellery, expect the following when selling your secondhand[1] item to a trader.

Expect between 20% and 25% of the new retail price in a shop (and the same relative to an insurance valuation if the valuation reflects the replacement price); between 25% and 50% of the *secondhand* retail price in an upmarket shop, antiques fair or antiques centre; between 50% and 80% of the secondhand retail price in a market, downmarket antiques centre or 'general' antiques fair.

All this is, of course, *very* approximate. If you *don't* get these percentages, it could be that the original purchase price of the item was too high or it could be that you are not being offered enough as a secondhand item (or it could be that my percentages are wrong).

SOME SELLING TIPS

Most days, in the shop, I would make an offer for an item and be told that my offer was low and that the man around the corner had offered more. The customer would return later in the day to sell the goods to me. Why? The man around the corner stuck by his valuation but was not, himself, prepared to buy the item. So ask if the buyer is prepared to buy at that price, for instance "...so if I call to see you at 2pm, will you give me that amount?" or "If I post the goods today, when will I get paid?"

When telephoning around for a scrap price, ask if the seller pays a percentage of the actual gold value. He probably does. But he won't necessarily want to tell you what it is. *If* he will give you this figure, you can calculate the amount he will pay at any time, either to sell your item another day or to sell to that trader on a regular basis. See the formulae on page 47.

When telephoning for a price on bullion (bars or coins) ask for the buying *and* selling price. The difference between buying and selling is called the 'spread', and will tell you the margin the dealer is working on. This will vary depending upon the total value of the transaction, and it will vary

---

[1] As far as jewellery is concerned it's 'secondhand' even if it's an unwanted Christmas present and has never been worn...perhaps, "pre-owned" would be a better term.

over the weeks and months.[1]

An example: three coin / bullion dealers. The first says that for a quantity of ten Sovereigns his buying price is £170.00 and his selling price (per coin) is £180.00. Maybe the price isn't right for you today, but it shows you the type of deal you'll get. The second quotes £150.00 / £200.00. Not so good. The third takes great offence at the question and wants to know if you are buying or selling. He isn't a real bullion dealer, you are asking the wrong person. Please do remember that you should get a good deal for two hundred coins and not such a good deal for two coins.

If you have had several offers, all at about the same price, and then receive an offer which is twice as high, it's probably a mistake so check it carefully otherwise you might find yourself travelling a great distance (or spending money on postage) only to be told – it's a mistake.

When selling by mail, check the company's terms and conditions, including the option to cancel the deal and have your goods back if the price drops by the time they receive the goods. If they quote you a price on a Monday but don't receive the goods until Thursday, the price is likely to have changed, if only slightly.[2]

IDENTIFICATION

When out selling, carry proof of identity. It is frustrating to spend all day hunting around for a good price only to find that nobody will buy because you have no identification. A letter from Aunt Agatha will not be accepted as identification and neither will a telephone number (some sellers would say to me: 'telephone this number and my mother will tell you this is me').

Until recently, buyers merely needed to know your identity so that *if* it turned out not to be your property to sell, the police are guaranteed to find you. Since then, a series of anti-money-laundering laws[3] have tightened up procedures. A buyer *should* not only check your identification but take photocopies of two documents.

---

[1] Dealers can work on tighter margins when the gold price is high and there's a high level of trade and money to be made, but they must be cautious when trade is bad and prices are depressed – they have to make a living *somehow*!

[2] You might be able to confirm a price on the phone (a 'deal' - you can't change your mind) or you might have to accept the price on the day it arrives, there's no standard procedure, you must ask

[3] Terrorism Act 2000, Proceeds of Crime Act 2002, and Money Laundering Regulations 2007

The first document must contain your photograph and / or signature and must be traceable, for instance:

- Cheque guarantee card / credit card / debit card
- Bank / Building Society / National Savings book
- Store Account Card (embossed, not a loyalty card)
- Passport (any nationality)
- Work Photo Pass if the company is nationally-known (i.e. the ID must be verifiable, not something you designed on a computer)

Examples of documents that are not acceptable:

- travel pass
- store loyalty card
- membership card for a club, gym, wholesaler, etc.

The second document must be proof of address and must be no more than three months old, for instance:

- Utility bill (not a mobile phone bill or store / charge card bill)
- Full driving License (must be accompanied by the counterpart driving licence D740 which is issued with the card)
- Credit card / bank / Building Society statement
- Council Tax payment book
- Council rent book

Examples of documents that are not acceptable:

- personal letter
- catalogue, circular or any un-dated, un-addressed general literature

One large high street chain of shops uses an ingenious system. You 'register' with them, they check your I.D. and then send a 'membership card' to your home address. You come back to sell the goods when you have the membership card.

Some buyers don't bother with most of this, but will, at least, insist on paying by cheque or bank transfer so that there is a 'paper trail' showing where the money has gone.

BUYING

Buying jewellery in London's Bond Street is certainly an experience not to be missed. Along with the best quality in the world, comes the very latest in fashion, and all served with a smile. Gold and silver is for wearing - if you like a piece of jewellery then the money spent is worth the pleasure it brings. Gold and silver has an advantage over most household objects: it has a high intrinsic value, but this is very much secondary to its main purpose as a fashion item.

Some people have the value-for-money bug. For them the hunting ground is not the high street shop but the junk shop, flea market or antiques fair. Many a secondhand bargain can be found and the shabbiest of items can be sent away for professional polishing. The cost is low and the result is an item as bright as the day it was made. That is the beauty of gold, it can always be polished to its original shine, see page 70.

It is possible to buy secondhand jewellery both to wear and for investment. For modern items this requires a lot of shopping around and forever being conscious of the value relative to the weight of gold or silver. A collection of jewellery of excellent value can be amassed providing that high fashion, fast service and free alterations are not expected. Buying on a weight basis has its rewards. It also brings its disasters: the biggest bargain in town is often the ugliest piece of jewellery that nobody else would buy. Antique and collectable jewellery requires more effort, scouring every junk shop, flea market, boot sale and antiques fair.

BUYING FROM RETAIL SHOPS

There are various types of retail outlets selling new jewellery, some of which you may not have thought of. There are the 'multiples' (eg. H Samuel and Ernest Jones[1]); department stores (eg. John Lewis, Debenhams); some of the supermarkets (eg. Tesco, Asda, Marks & Spencer); semi-wholesale stores (eg. Costco); catalogue stores (eg. Argos, Empire, Littlewoods).

Today's style tends to be 'open plan' where the customer is 'invited' to wander in and browse the museum-style cabinets. Some offer extra

---

[1] These are part of the Signet group. In the USA they are called Kay Jewellers and Jared. Some other 'names' that have hundreds of branches throughout the UK are F Hinds, Goldsmiths, Warren James.

services such as providing a working jeweller[1] on the premises.

There are also many thousands of family jewellers. Some of these are very small (maybe a unit in a market hall) and some are larger (maybe four shops in three towns). Here the emphasis is less on 'hard sell' and more on giving the best service and good advice, because they are experts. They may get goods especially to show you, may arrange exchanges or credits if you are not happy, may have a custom-design service, may have specialist repair services or may have contacts who can find you antique jewellery or coins. For all of this the price may be a little higher than at the larger shops...though not necessarily as they *will* be aware of the competition from other shops.

There are two areas in the UK which abound with jewellery shops: the 'Jewellery Quarters' of London and Birmingham. In London, Hatton Garden (see www.hatton-garden.net); in Birmingham, Hockley (see www.the-quarter.com). Each has enough shops for a week's window shopping. These districts also have workshops for both repairing and manufacturing, often with small retail outlets attached. The most exclusive jewellery shops (including antiques specialists) can be found in London's Bond Street.

JUNK SHOPS AND ANTIQUES SHOPS

Antiques shops often breed. Evidence of this can be seen in The Lanes in Brighton, where hundreds of antiques shops are clustered together in a maze of winding lanes, or in the Cotswold villages where antiques shops outnumber food shops. Specialist antiques shops buy and sell only high quality goods. These are the places to find good quality Georgian and Victorian jewellery, high quality gemstones and 'named' antique silver.

The average antiques shop may have a large selection of 'everyday' jewellery at greatly reduced price tucked away in dusty showcases at the back of the shop; the down-market antiques or junk shop may also have jewellery, it is always worth asking if there is anything which has just come in and has not been put on display.

Many junk shops deal in furniture and other large items. They advertise in local newspapers under 'HOUSE CLEARANCES' - they will empty entire houses of their contents when someone emigrates, moves to a smaller

---

[1] I took a friend's neck chain to be repaired and was surprised to be told it would take a week. When I questioned this, he said, "I do have other things to do you know!" The idea of the multi-service jewellery shop is good but don't assume the service will be faster than a shop that sends goods away.

house or dies. Along with furniture they also buy small items ('smalls') including gold and silver. If there is a junk shop near you it may be worth popping in regularly since gold and silver are often sold to the first dealer who calls and not put on display.

PAWNBROKERS

Pawnbrokers don't actually 'buy' goods. They lend money, taking the goods as security, then (within an agreed time) you pay the money back plus interest, and they give you the goods back. If you don't claim the goods, the Pawnbroker recovers the money by selling them. Theoretically, this can involve any high-value item, even cars. In practice pawnbrokers only have room to store small items, and gold and silver is ideal.

The old image of the Dickensian pawnbroker[1] is long gone. Today pawnbrokers are more like banks, with bank counters behind which are the gold-testing and weighing equipment, and they are now used by everyone from the near-destitute pawning a wedding ring to the businessman pawning his Rolex watch.

THE ALL-PURPOSE HIGH STREET
SECONDHAND / LOANS SHOPS

The main purpose of these shops is to offer cheque-cashing services, instant loans and foreign currency but they also buy scrap and jewellery, and some offer the saleable items in their shops and on their websites. Options are: to order the item by post, to call in at the branch, or to enter into an auction, similar to eBay.

A glance at their websites indicates that they tend to sell heavier items for twice the actual gold value, a good price compared with buying new, a bad price compared with selling scrap, so, I suppose, on average, the price is about right. For antique items you may prefer to buy at antiques shops, fairs and centres.

See Cash Converters (www.cashconverters.co.uk, over 170 shops) and Cash Generator (www.cashgenerator.co.uk, over 100 shops).

---

[1] The nursery rhyme *Half a Pound of Twopenny Rice* contains the words, *Pop goes the Weasel*. To 'pop' means to pawn, and a weasel was a coat (in Cockney rhyming slang, Weasel and Stoat)...or it may have been a silk-maker's bobbin.

JUMBLE SALES AND GARAGE SALES

Jumble sales raise money for charity: goods are donated and sold at a sale which lasts no more than a couple of hours, offering mostly clothes but also books, games and toys and bric-a-brac. Prices are at the discretion of the stall-minder, usually 20p to £1.00 per item. Jumble sales are advertised in local newspapers and on posters displayed in local shops.

Every dedicated jumble-sale-goer has a story about a 15ct-and-diamond Victorian brooch which cost £1.00 at the bric-a-brac stall. If you visit two or three jumble sales a week for a number of years you are certain to find such a bargain one day, but the 'bargain' is likely to have cost you several hundred hours of searching. As a sport, jumble-sale-going is equal to the first day at the sales for thrills - the mad scramble at the bric-a-brac stall, dozens of hands grabbing at goods, the 'dealer' competing with the poor, it's more humane than blood sports, but only slightly.

Jumble sales are unknown in the United States where the garage sale (or yard sale) is common. Garage sales are not so common in the United Kingdom. As with the jumble sale, unwanted household items are sold, but unlike the jumble sale the prices tend to be more than nominal. The only time you are likely to have luck is if the owners are emigrating and large items *must* be sold by a certain date, but don't get too excited, items of gold and silver are small and there is not likely to be a panic to sell them.

BOOT SALES

A boot sale is a sale of goods sold from the boots of cars (or, rather, from a table set up by the car). Small boot sales organised by local charities attract no more than a couple of dozen cars and often no more than a couple of dozen customers. Large boot sales which are held regularly attract hundreds of sellers and thousands of customers. Amidst the largest array of junk you are ever likely to see, will be some gold and silver. Sellers of jewellery (usually their own treasured possessions) usually base their prices on the original retail price - far too much, most items are worth only scrap value.

The boot sale season was once seasonal, flourishing in the summer and gradually dying off in the winter. Boot sales now seem to be an all-the-year-round activity, only to be cancelled in the event of thick snow or fog or continuous torrential rain...and even then *some* people turn up.

My only prejudice against boot sales is that the standard of honesty on the part of the sellers (mostly private sellers, not traders) is poor. They will quite happily describe gold plated costume jewellery as 'genuine hallmarked gold' or worn and worthless coins as 'in perfect condition and very valuable'. You cannot return goods bought from private individuals and you have few of the rights afforded by law when buying from a trader.

However, many professional traders sell at boot sales too. They might be 'clearing' end of lines or selling left-over antiques from 'job lots' or slightly damaged items or items they've had in stock too long and which are now 'written off' in the books, or items they don't normally deal in and don't understand - there are many reasons professional traders sell at boot sales. Some like to pretend they are not traders, to encourage the 'bargain hunters'[1] while others make it obvious they are professional traders by offering their business card to anyone who takes the slightest interest.

So how do you *know* if someone is a professional trader or a purely 'private' person? You should recognise them by the unusually 'high quality' or 'interesting' items on the table, compared with the pure unadulterated junk all around (and a battered Volvo with a huge roof rack is also a sign of a trader). You are not so likely to pick up that bargain of a lifetime, but you are more likely to find something worth buying at the 'right' price.

ANTIQUES FAIRS AND MARKETS: THE PROFESSIONALS AND THE DABBLERS

Antiques fairs vary in quality from downmarket (any mixture of 'antiques' fair and 'flea' market) to fairs so renowned that they are reviewed on national television - and with this mix of fairs comes a mix of sellers, from part-timers (dabblers) who sell at weekend and bank holiday fairs, to full-timers (including antiques companies, galleries and fine art dealers).

Personally, I find fairs with a high proportion of dabblers frustrating places to buy, half the time you can buy the same item for less money from any high street shop.

---

[1] It's all a matter of psychology - some buyers think professional traders must, automatically, be too expensive so the professional trader goes to great lengths to make the table look messy and to plead ignorance whenever they are asked for more information about the items. At the same time, there are sellers who want their professionalism and honesty to stand out amidst all the 'amateurs'.

Top antiques fairs

At these fairs a significant number of stalls specialise in jewellery. Some are held in smart hotels, some in small exhibition halls, and they provide up-market goods of a standard every bit as high as Bond Street. The best are carefully vetted[1] by the organisers to ensure that every item is antique and abides by the advertised 'dateline' eg. 'DATELINE 1930' or 'DATELINE 1870'. The top fairs are internationally known and are even reviewed in the national press and on television.

I reviewed some of these fairs when I wrote a column for an antiques newspaper, and it was a real eye-opener! On the one hand, prices were four to eight times more than the prices I charged when selling to the trade. On the other hand every item was perfect and every item was unique. One stand had just five items for sale, the seller had flown in from New York for the day and the items were priced from £15,000 to £25,000.

Size can be anywhere from 200 stands at an exhibition hall or large hotel, to 20 in a room in a stately home. The sellers here *will* be professional traders, first because they need to know what they're doing, secondly because the organisers need to know they know what they're doing, and thirdly because the rent for the stall (or unit) will be thousands of pounds.

Upmarket antiques fairs

These are held in hotels and exhibition halls but, unlike the 'top' fairs do not have enforced datelines or vetting committees or reviews on television, and so the quality is more variable. Sometimes the only difference between these and a 'general ' antiques fair is that they are in a prime tourist location and in a posh venue where prices are high. Size can be anywhere from 200 stands at an exhibition hall or large hotel, to 20 in a village hall. The sellers are *mostly* (but not entirely) professional traders.

General Antiques Fairs

Many antiques fairs are to be found in large halls, stately homes (and their grounds), exhibition centres, town halls and community centres, usually on Saturdays, Sundays or Bank Holidays. Some are held monthly, many of the larger fairs are held quarterly, twice-yearly or annually. Size,

---

[1] Before the fair opens a 'vetting committee' checks the standard of goods on every single stand, not only for age but also for condition, eg. items described as 'original' must not have been altered. This is very rare in the case of gold and silver items because they *do* wear out or get broken over the years and *will* have been repaired several times.

between 50 and 300 stands; quality, from junk to the very best; availability of gold and silver, plentiful. These are held on weekends or Bank Holidays to attract private buyers (though there will always be a special 'early entry – higher entry price' for trade buyers) – these fairs *do* attract a significant number of sellers who are dabblers but many professional traders too.

Trade Antiques Fairs

There are, in Britain, a handful of large 'trade' antiques fairs, each held just a few times a year, most lasting two days midweek. The first day is reserved for stallholders to set up their stand (at some fairs there's a £10.00 or £20.00 early-entry charge), the second day is open to the trade and the public. 'Trade' comprises anyone (trade or public) eager enough to get up very early and pay a high entrance fee. These fairs tend to be large, from 300 to 1000 stalls, and are held on agricultural showgrounds or disused airfields.

The fair held at the Newark & Notts. Agricultural Showground, for instance, averages 1,000 stands. Don't worry, therefore, about missing bargains if you can't get in early. These fairs are so vast that the trade buyers couldn't possibly *see* all the bargains, let alone buy them. Most sellers are professionals (or, these days, the recently unemployed embarking upon a new career), if only because the fairs are held midweek when many people are at work.

Trade Markets

Another hunting ground for the professional buyer and avid bargain hunter is the early morning market, seemingly ordinary markets in the middle of the day but bustling trade markets very early in the morning.

Clusters of buyers cram around the stalls and there's the fast patter of numbers as the seller gives prices and the buyers say 'yes' or 'no' to each item, a far cry from the genteel chat of a shop or antiques fair. Add to this the fact that for most of the year it will be dark and you will be buying by torchlight – not a way to buy unless you know what you are doing. Not all markets are outdoors, some are held in market halls which have the advantage of proper lighting, though not necessarily heating.

Examples are: Bermondsey, near London Bridge (now revamped following five years of rebuilding work); Kempton[1] on the first and last

---

[1] Its full name is Sunbury Antiques Market at Kempton Park Racecourse, Surrey

Tuesday of the month; and Birmingham Rag Market[1] about ten times per year on a Wednesday. One advantage of these markets is that entrance for the buyers is free. Another advantage is that you can visit early and be back in the office or shop in time for lunch. You can, of course, visit at any time. You don't have to be there early in the morning but traders do tend to get obsessive about getting 'first pick' of the goodies for sale.

Flea Markets

These are very slightly up-market versions of boot sales and are held indoors. The percentage of professional sellers is higher than at a boot sale and that means that there are more goods of a standard worth buying. Flea markets are often added to another event, eg. 'BOOT SALE AND FLEA MARKET': selling is from the boots of cars outdoors and from tables indoors; or 'ANTIQUES FAIR AND FLEA MARKET': an antiques fair in the main hall and junk in a side room. In a poorly organised 'ANTIQUES FAIR AND FLEA MARKET' the junk will be in the main hall and it's up to you to try and find an antique in the side room. Flea markets are held in church halls, village halls or Scout huts and therefore tend to be small. The chances of finding gold and silver at a flea market are higher than at a jumble sale or boot sale...slightly.

MAIL ORDER

Many new items appear in mail order catalogues at remarkably cheap prices. Some items are excellent value for money, others are not. Look at photographs carefully, they can be deceptive, especially since jewellery and medallions are photographed against plain velvet backgrounds which give no indication of size. Many diamond rings are made of 9ct gold (diamonds of any value merit 18ct gold settings) and the diamonds themselves may be no more than the size of pinpricks. Also, read the text carefully to see if bangles are made of solid gold or hollow gold (i.e. gold tubing) - both will look the same in a photograph but one will be heavier than the other.

If you reply to advertisements in newspapers, magazines or mail order catalogues, you have a great many rights[2]. The advertiser has to agree to send an acknowledgement of order, to send the goods within twenty

---

[1] The organisers advertise it as 'Big Brum', it used to be called The Rag Market. Its real name is St Martin's Market, it's opposite St Martin's Church at the Bull Ring. Do not confuse this with the 'big' venue in Birmingham (which often holds large antiques fairs) the National Exhibition Centre (NEC)

[2] The seller must be *Trade* (not a private individual) and the advert / catalogue must include prices and invite you to send money,

eight days and to give you seven days to decide if you are happy with the goods.[1] Some advertisers make a feature of this condition (IF, FOR WHATEVER REASON, YOU ARE NOT SATISFIED WITH THE GOODS, WE GUARANTEE TO REFUND YOUR MONEY!), other advertisers don't mention the subject hoping that it simply won't occur to the buyer that he can return goods. Do read the terms & conditions, you will almost certainly have to return the item 'in saleable condition' and you will probably have to pay the postage[2].

None of these rights apply if you are buying from a private individual. In Small Ads there should be a letter 'T' for Trade at the end of each advertisement to denote *Trade Seller*.

AUCTIONS

Only the largest and most prestigious of auction rooms sell works of art that hit the news headlines. Most sell lesser goods, mostly for traders to resell, and the quality varies from 'average' to 'junk'. Small auctions are the best places for finding both bargains and curios. Because general auctions sell anything and everything, it can easily happen that on that particular day you are the only person who is after gold and silver - suddenly you are the gold and silver expert in a room full of specialists in other subjects.

It is through auctions that bankrupt stock, the contents of entire houses, personal collections, and items from traders are sold. Anyone can buy at auction. The private buyer, therefore, has an advantage over the dealer since a dealer will stop bidding when he cannot see himself making a profit. Private buyers who spend large amounts of money and prevent the professional traders from buying the best goods are very popular with the sellers...and very unpopular with the professional buyers. But it can backfire because sometimes the professional bidders 'gang up' on a private bidder. Realising that a private buyer is outbidding them, the professional bidders will use their experience to bid rapidly to create great excitement, then all stop suddenly leaving the private buyer with a ridiculously high winning bid. No conspiracy is involved, the entire process is spontaneous.

So *are* auctions good places to buy? Often, but not always. Occasionally the auction houses play The Auction Game. It goes like this.

---

[1] Many (including ourselves) extend this to 14 days

[2] This is no different from buying in a shop. Try asking them to refund your bus fair or petrol money!

A man spends his entire life collecting junk. When he dies the estate goes to auction. How on earth can the auctioneers sell three warehouses full of junk? This is how. They mount a massive publicity campaign featuring the one-time eccentric who collected junk. The media has a field day, the one-time eccentric becomes famous and the auction attracts would-be antiques collectors from all over the country. In the fever and excitement of the sale, the prices bid are several times the true market price. In reality it will take many generations before the 'junk' becomes 'antique'.

A variation on this theme is the publicising of a famous collection. There may be only twenty wealthy collectors of gold plated cheese wrappers in the world; and if the largest collection of gold plated cheese wrappers is to be auctioned, it follows that the only way to attract a good price is to find the twenty collectors. Unlike the case of selling junk, the rare collection *is* rare, you will not see gold plated cheese wrappers in every jewellers and antiques shop in the country. As for their worth, that is an unknown quantity. In a few year's time the same collection will be worth even more if there are even more wealthy collectors, if not, it will be worth less. My example of gold plated cheese wrappers is silly, please substitute your own examples: the rarest collection of hand-made watches, gold eggs, a collection of jewellery belonging to a member of the royal family, the treasure from a sunken ship...

Auctions are time consuming. There may be two hours of bidding for furniture and bric-a-brac before the few gold and silver items are bid, and if someone else bids higher than you the entire afternoon becomes a waste of time. Sometimes the auction catalogue's 'estimate' (the auctioneer's estimate of selling value) is very low, encouraging potential buyers to give up their time and travel a long distance to attend the auction, then it is revealed that the 'reserve price' (the minimum price the seller will accept) is far above this[1] and the price eventually bid may be higher still. This can make a wasted journey to an auction even more frustrating.

The porters can advise as to when an item will be bid - it is quite permissible to arrive late (or to go out for a coffee and come back later). Always go along to view the items before the auction and try not to buy on impulse. As you view, mark the prices you are prepared to pay by each lot number in the catalogue, then when you are bidding, *stick to these*

---

[1] Although not illegal in the UK (in New York the reserve price may not exceed the top estimate) the practice is 'frowned upon'.

prices (auctions are also excellent places to sell items for the simple reason that bidders get carried away and bid too high).

The catalogue is also useful for waving vigorously in the air the first time you start to bid. In this way you will attract the auctioneer's attention, otherwise he will assume you are waving to a friend or scratching your nose. Once you have entered the bidding the auctioneer will know you are there to buy and not just to watch and he will keep an eye on you, then a mere nod of the head or raising of a finger will suffice each time you bid. Once you have successfully bid for an item the auctioneer will shout 'NAME?' and you will should out a name. If your own name is too long for the auctioneer to understand then use a shorter name for the day. In many auction rooms bidders register and are supplied with a 'paddle' (like a small rowing boat paddle) on which there is a number. It is raised in the air, making it easier for the auctioneer to see who is bidding.

The procedure after making a successful bid varies. Sometimes a deposit must be paid, sometimes the goods can be paid for in full and taken away, sometimes payment is made after the auction and the goods collected at any time that day or the next - the details will be in the catalogue. Also in the catalogue will be details of extra charges, including a 12% to 25% (+ VAT) buyer's premium (the commission the auction house takes as profit). There may be additional charges such as a charge for putting a photograph of your item into the catalogue. Do not, therefore, bid 'a good buying price', bid that price less the buyer's premium.

An auction is not just a sale. Traders meet other traders, make contacts, exchange gossip and, most important of all, see how much items are selling for...and who is buying them...and why. It is because of auctions that many traders know how much to pay for items they have never bought before - they can seen how much the items are selling for at auction; and these prices *are* the actual prices paid by traders, not hypothetical prices quoted in catalogues. In addition to learning prices, traders can see *who* is bidding and reach conclusions: why is Mr Jones from the antiques shop in the High Street bidding so much for early gold sovereigns?...why is Miss Higgins buying enamelled silver brooches just before her trip to Japan?...maybe there's a craze for silver *mizpah*[1] brooches in the United States...or Italian speculators are buying English gold coins...or English students are buying Edwardian costume jewellery...or a strong US dollar is attracting American buyers.... Such information is valuable.

---

[1] This word (on jewellery, typically Victorian) originates from the Bible (Genesis 31) and means "The Lord watch between me and thee when we are absent one from another".

SOME TIPS WHEN BUYING

WHY SO EXPENSIVE? WHY SO CHEAP?

Very often you will look at goods and become puzzled. You will be puzzled by the price. You will say to yourself: why is this item so expensive? or why is this item so cheap? There are some obvious possibilities: the seller has made a mistake and mis-labelled the item; you have made a mistake and don't realise the true worth; the seller thinks the item is hideous and is asking a low price while you think the item is beautiful and should be worth more...or vice versa. There are many other reasons why gold and silver can be 'too cheap' or 'too expensive' and knowing the reasons can help you find a bargain or avoid a 'rip-off'.

COMPARE LIKE WITH LIKE

When comparing prices of jewellery check the carat, an 18ct bracelet will be more expensive than the identical bracelet made of 9ct. Check the weight, two chains may appear the same but one may be 20% lighter than the other, or one may be solid and the other made of hollow tubing.

If you are accustomed to buying in boot sales, a high street shop will seem expensive. If you always buy at high street shops in your local town then the shops of London's Bond Street will seem expensive. Conversely, a visit to a large antiques fair will provide many surprises if you have only ever shopped at the large 'multiple' jewellery shops; and at a local flea market you *may* see a bargain that will make your eyes pop out; or you may find so much worthless junk that you rush straight back to your favourite high street shop.

WHY SO CHEAP?

Mr Jones is a trader who is offered 500 gold medallions at an amount nominally over the gold price. He is offered the medallions because the manufacturers are closing down and are pleased to get more than the scrap price. Mr Jones needs £37,500.00 to buy these but he can only afford £7,500.00 per month, so he agrees to buy a hundred each month for five months. Mr Jones now *must* sell enough each month to pay for the next batch. He is happy that one day he will have a few which he can afford to sell at a good profit, meanwhile he must sell them quickly and so offers them at a low price - they are a bargain.

Mr Smith is another trader in a shop nearby. Mr Smith is in a similar situation, having been offered a similar batch of medallions. Mr Smith, however, can afford to spend £37,500.00 all at once. He then places large advertisements in newspapers offering the medallions at a high price. Several months later he has sold most of the medallions, his advertising campaign has finished and he has only a few remaining. Mr Smith is no longer interested in medallions and so sells his remaining stock at a very low price - they are a bargain.

My point is that there can be quite genuine reasons for identical items varying in price, and if you were to say to Mr Smith, "Why are you so much more expensive than Mr Jones?" he will simply shrug his shoulders...because it's just too complicated to explain.

There are simpler reasons why gold and silver items can be cheap (though never below the scrap price): liquidators must sell bankrupt stock at a low price; after a flood or fire entire crates of goods may be 'written off' by insurer's loss adjusters and sold at a low price; a jeweller may retire and sell his business and the new owners may simply not want some of the stock, they would rather sell it at a very low price and use the money to buy different stock.

There is also the matter of fashion, because most items of jewellery are 'fashion items'.

Fashions change: if silver razor blades and gold safety pins are out of fashion then any you find should be very cheap, and if you still have them when they come back into fashion you could resell them for a large profit...or, more likely, the person with the biggest smile will be the seller, having found someone silly enough to buy the 'bargains'.

Fashion is also cultural. My bosses in the jewellers shop bought a *huge* 18ct ring with *bright* red and blue and green stones. The scrap value was high and I advised them to scrap it, since the overall appearance was of something from a Christmas Cracker, maybe it would appeal to a six-year-old with very large hands, but not a grownup. They disagreed with me, and they were the bosses, and they put it in the window. Within the day a large Nigerian lady had bought it. To my English eye it was ostentatious and gaudy, to an African eye it was truly beautiful...or, at least, that's what I assume.

If you are buying from someone who appears to be a professional trader yet is selling gold and silver for less than the scrap price you *may* have found a bargain - maybe the seller has miscalculated the price. If the items are quite definitely being offered at less than the scrap price, regard the entire transaction as suspicious - gold and silver have a definite scrap value and *no* genuine trader sells for below the price he can get as scrap.

Do be very careful when buying from private buyers - if they tell you their jewellery is 18ct gold and you part with money only to find it is 18ct gold plated, you are most unlikely to get your money back.

BEWARE OF OVER-ENTHUSIASTIC SALESMEN

Wherever you are buying, the chances are that you will be confronted by a salesman. The law regarding correct descriptions of goods is strict but it is well nigh impossible to prove that you were misled by what you were told on the spur of the moment. In the case of boot sales and flea markets it may be difficult to find the seller even if you could prove that you were misled.

If you are spending a lot of money at a market or fair, get a receipt and *read it* (to check that it is correct) before you leave. Most professional antiques traders and market traders will give receipts, even from a market stall providing they are not too busy (they may ask you to come back in a few minutes when they have time to find their receipt book). In any regular market make a note of the stall number or position so that you can find that stall again. At a boot sale make a note of the car registration number. You should automatically be given a receipt in a shop, if not, ask for one, and *don't lose it.* Every shop worker will tell you that whenever a customer returns querying a sale of a few days earlier, it is quite certain that the shop assistant who sold the item is not in that day, that the customer can't find the receipt, that the copy has been sent to the accounts department and that the customer wants the matter sorted out within five minutes.

If you are giving an item as a present and are not sure if the recipient will like it, ask the seller if they can change it for something else - don't assume that they can. If the seller says yes, get a receipt, seal it in an envelope and give it with the present. The recipient need never look at the receipt but at least they have proof of purchase should they wish to change the item[1].

Most important of all, listen to what the seller says. Professional sellers *do* tend to be honest and give very precise information but private sellers

---

[1] Legally, the original purchaser must pursue the matter, though the shop will not know (or care) who that was...unless it had been paid by credit card, in which case the shopkeeper will want to refund the money for the original purchase back to the original credit card, then ask you how you wish to pay for the new purchase.

often 'make it up as they go along.' For instance:

THIS ITEM IS PLATED WITH 100 PER CENT GENUINE 18CT GOLD
- *quite worthy as costume jewellery no doubt, but not gold.*

GIVEN TIME THIS SILVER CHAIN WILL APPRECIATE IN VALUE
- *Yes, given a few hundred years*

A GOOD DIAMOND IS A GOOD INVESTMENT
- *unlikely*

THESE STONES ARE GUARANTEED REAL
- *real what? Real synthetic spinel? Real cubic zirconia?*

I DON'T KNOW HOW OLD THIS RING IS BUT IT CERTAINLY ISN'T NEW.
- *but it's certainly not antique...in fact it's an unwanted present from last Christmas.*

IT'S QUITE OLD BUT I DON'T KNOW HOW OLD
- *It's very old, maybe five or ten years old...but not antique*

THEY DON'T MAKE THESE ANY MORE, THEY'RE BECOMING QUITE RARE
- *They were discontinued because nobody would buy them*

IT MAY BE OVER TWO HUNDRED YEARS OLD
- *or it may not be*

IF YOU ARE NOT SATISFIED JUST COME BACK NEXT WEEK
...Why? - because the seller is emigrating on Friday?
...or...Yes, bring it back, you may exchange it for something else, but no refund will be given

IT'S ANTIQUE-Y
- *Is that antique-ish or antique-like or simply modern*

Traders (honest as they tend to be) aren't obliged to offer information. Many (and I must confess, I am one of these) say little or nothing as the *customer* tells the *trader* about the item. The customer assumes many things he is not told and assumes the trader agrees. The moral: don't show off your knowledge, the trader will eagerly give you information if you take the trouble to listen. Then, if you are misled, you have good cause to complain. If you do have cause to return an item, start by being polite, traders are only human and do make mistakes occasionally, and when they do, their embarrassment is such that they will often do anything (within reason) to make amends and keep your custom.

DISCOUNTS

The British do not generally haggle over prices. I once found myself at the checkout of a small food shop with a bill for £5.01 and only a £50.00 note, and there was no change in the till. I was in a hurry and so the obvious solution occurred to me: I asked for a 1p discount. At this suggestion the checkout girl turned pale with fright - it is not acceptable to ask for a discount in most shops.

So when is it polite to ask for a discount? If you walk into a high street jewellers, look at a gold chain priced at £120.00 and say 'I'll give you ninety quid!' - the shopkeeper will not respond enthusiastically. *However,* shop assistants in the centre of large cities are quite used to African and Asian customers haggling, and may even have added an extra 10% onto the tag price so that they can instantly give a 10% discount on any sale. This will not be the case in areas where overseas tourists are not common. The general rule, in a shop, is that if you are spending a large amount of money you have bargaining power. If you are about to spend £5,000 or £10,000 on a diamond necklace the shopkeeper will almost certainly be willing to give a discount rather than lose the sale; if you are spending £62.50, the shopkeeper may prefer to lose the sale than cut his profit.

At fairs and markets haggling is commonplace, but to be effective it must be low-key. Market traders know that Italian buyers have an abrupt style, offering half the asking price and then haggling, Mediterranean-style, hoping for a compromise. The British are generally more subdued, they ask for sensible discounts and as a result are more likely to have their offer accepted. Not having your offer accepted does not mean you can't buy at the full price. I have seen many a bargain missed simply because the trader would not give a discount - if you really like a piece of gold or silver and the price seems reasonable (or if you are a trader and *can* make a profit) then don't play haggling games - BUY IT!

BUYING AND SELLING FOR PROFIT

The previous sections include *Buying* (where to buy, what you get, and how much you might pay) and *Selling* (different methods of selling, where to get the best price) – assuming you are looking for a specific item to buy for yourself (or as a present) or a good price to get for your own gold and silver. This section is very specifically for the trader whose aim is to make a profit.

To buy and sell for profit is infinitely more difficult than just buying or just selling. There are three ways of trading: by buying at the lower price from the public and selling at a higher price to the trade (eg. secondhand goods); by buying at the lower price from the trade and selling at the a higher price to the public (eg. new items); by buying from the trade and selling to the trade. This last is the most difficult. Traders know the prices of the goods they deal with and these prices do not vary greatly. The result is that profits to be made by buying and selling within the trade are very small, you might be working on a markup of around 10% and you must know the subject well enough to know that you will make that 10% and not lose 10%.

PART TIME

To sell the occasional piece of jewellery see page 77. To sell a large collection or to sell goods which you have bought especially for resale there are various options: sell them privately to friends or through newspaper advertisements; put them into auction; rent a stall at a market or fair, or share one with a friend. Combined with any of these is the option of being a part time 'runner' – running from fair to market to auction to private customer, buying and selling wherever you can.

These are the typical rents charged for stalls[1] and pitches.[2] A boot sale £8.00 to £15.00; at a flea market, small provincial antiques fair or street market £12.00 to £20.00; at a smart hotel antiques fair or at the larger (including midweek 'trade') fairs £40.00 to £100.00; at a large up-market stand-fitted[3] fair lasting two or three days, a few hundred pounds; at a

---

[1] At an antiques fair you get one table 2ft X 6ft, at a 'traditional' council-run street market the stall can be as large as 2½ft X 7ft. Sometimes there is extra space around it to set up additional tables, often there is not.

[2] A space, typically 20ft X 20ft, no tables or chairs are provided

[3] A partitioned area in the style of a Trade Exhibition, usually with a board above the entrance naming the exhibitor, often with cabinets and shelves rather than just tables.

large and prestigious top-quality vetted fair lasting a few days, a few thousand pounds.

Visit each market or fair first to see if it is suitable for your standard of goods, have a chat with the organiser to find out the rent and future dates and chat to stallholders[1]. If you are impressed, book a stall for the next time. You cannot expect to make a profit at the first few events, all your money will be put back into stock.

If your 'fling' at selling gold and silver is a one-off attempt to sell your own goods then there is no 'profit' to be made. If you enjoy the day but don't sell anything, try again another day with your prices slightly lower. If you must have cash that same day, then you will have to lower the prices by the hour until someone buys from you. Most important of all, relax and enjoy the day. There is nothing better than company and sunshine at a boot sale on a summer's afternoon,[2] or pleasant company and tea in a warm hall at an antiques fair on a cold winter morning. Returning home with some pocket money makes the day all the more enjoyable.

FULL TIME - NEW GOODS

The reason why new jewellery can be expensive is that overheads are high. Many a time an enthusiastic would-be jeweller has set up shop only to find that there are so many overheads he has no money left to buy stock. Not only are there the usual expenses of rent, rates, maintenance and everyday bills but there are also extra costs. Insurance is particularly high and the insurers may insist that several thousand pounds be spent on safes, grills and alarms. Many insurance companies also insist on there being two or three members of staff present at all times. This means that it is difficult to start up a shop on the cheap, using, for instance, just yourself and a friend as staff - you may have to employ full time staff from the very start. Overheads *excluding* wages can be a few hundred pounds per day for a tiny shop in a city centre. This means that your *profit* per day must be high enough to cover that, *plus* wages for staff, and there must be enough money left over (from the profit) to buy extra stock *and* have enough money left over to live on.

In terms of starting a business, dealing in gold and silver is no different from starting any other business, you will need to produce a business

---

[1] The standard question I always ask is, "How's it going?" or "How's it been today?". If everyone I ask raises their eyebrows in despair and grunts or gives a non-committal reply, then the signs are not good; if answers vary from 'OK' to 'Good' then it looks promising; if some react with despair and some with enthusiasm, I must make my own judgement.
[2] But not according to my wife.

plan, work out your cash flow, raise money, organise incidentals like insurance, security, premises and maybe staff. The government organisation Business Link will help, they not only give general advice but organise government-sponsored courses. This and other job-related government agencies can be found at www.bis.gov.uk[1].

FULL TIME - SECONDHAND OR ANTIQUE GOODS

From Home or as a 'Runner'

The antiques trade is made up of many thousands of one-man businesses, the owners working from home, so this is a good place to start. Customers *will* want to visit (to buy or to sell) and one-man-traders *are* very shy about giving out their home address. This is partly for security reasons and partly because you are not really supposed to trade from home.

Many homes have what are known as *restrictive covenants*[2] forbidding you from trading from home. However, they are not enforced unless neighbours complain. So be discreet. Do not put up a large notice reading, *Old Jewellery Wanted* or invite callers at unusual hours.

A great many traders work from home, and they *are* full time professional traders using every 'channel' of buying and selling. For instance, buying at auction one day (see page 98), buying and selling at a fair or market another day (see page 94), trawling the antiques shops and centres another day (see below). There's a name for running about between shops and fairs and markets and dealers: a 'runner'. Runners do not need premises, they spend their days running about and, ideally, they end each day (or week) with the profit of their labours and don't accumulate stock.

---

[1] For instance, www.businesslink.gov.uk, www.skillsfundingagency.bis.gov.uk and www.direct.gov.uk/en/EducationAndLearning. But the level of help for new businesses does change with the political mood, so these website addresses are liable to change.

[2] Details of restrictive covenants for a property are available, for a small fee, from the Land Registry. There are many companies offering services based on Land Registry information, go to the *actual* Land Registry at www.landreg.gov.uk.

An Antiques Centre or Antiques Warehouse

One step up from working from home is to use an Antiques Centre. You pay a monthly rent for space (anything from a small showcase to a large counter), customers who are interested in your items ask the man at the desk to show them (he has the key), they pay at the checkout along with all their other purchases, the Centre's owner (or Accounts Department if it's large) sends you a cheque each month[1]. You can change the stock as often as you like, in fact the owner prefers you to change the stock as often as possible, otherwise the entire Centre starts to look stale.

The advantage of using a centre is that you have an address to print on visiting cards and somewhere where customers can view your new stock or bring items to sell. Do make sure they have a secure system for accepting post so that you can buy by mail.

A variation is the Antiques Warehouse. The principle is the same (dealers rent space) but it *will* be a warehouse rather than retail units, the aim being to fill containers with furniture rather than sell individual items, and so not the ideal place to sell gold and silver.

Offices, Industrial Units

If most of your business is going to be at the antiques fairs or by mail or by word of mouth, then any office will do, in an office block, above a shop, in the corner of a friend's warehouse, it really doesn't matter, you don't need to rent a shop in a high street.

Another option is a unit on an industrial estate, these vary from small (a table and chair, a telephone and a set of shelves) to large (large enough to employ several dozen people).

---

[1] Some centres deduct a fee (commission) in addition to the rent, this being to pay for the staff that work at the checkout desk and generally look after the Centre. Other centres don't employ staff to do this and don't charge commission, the dealers who rent the space have to take turns on the desk.

TIPS

To buy and sell gold and silver successfully you must:

Have a 'feel' for what is just coming into fashion *and* what is going out of fashion. If, for instance, you start by buying and selling gold pocket watches and the fashion for pocket watches ends you will find yourself with dozens of watches nobody will buy and no money to buy more stock. Values may, of course, rise. If you have unlimited money you can buy 'junk' and hope it becomes 'antique' but you will have to spend thousands of pounds and wait years never knowing which items will become valuable and which will remain junk. Few traders can afford to gamble in this way.

Be prepared to change with the fashion. You may be a pearl merchant this year, sell marcasite rings next year and Edwardian costume jewellery the next. Your aim *is* to become a knowledgeable all-rounder, a true expert in all things gold and silver...eventually.

All this takes time. Be prepared to spend a while learning each time you move into a new field, preferably a few weeks rather than a few months. This means that the first few of each new item you buy and sell you may not make a profit, and may make a loss. Learning is very expensive.

Have money to buy stock *and* travel around the country to find it (you will need a car). You will also have to pay rent for stalls or rent a shop or office. You may need the help of a bank manager and he will want evidence that you can handle the money he lends you as well as the gold and silver you are dealing with.

Be prepared to work unusual hours. Even if you have a shop which is open during shop hours you will still have to compete with other traders in the early hours of cold winter mornings in order to buy stock, or travel hundreds of miles to a good trade fair.

THE ART OF HAGGLING

When you are buying a secondhand item, think hard, decide how much you would like to pay, *then* ask the price. If the price is far too high, be polite, say thank you, walk on. If the price is 'close', ask for a discount, play it by ear, see if you can agree a price that gives you a good enough profit. If the price quoted is *lower* than you had thought, still ask for a discount, it's always worth asking, but if you think you can make a profit, buy it anyway. You are not buying on the basis of a percentage discount, you are buying because you are a trader and can make a profit.

When you buy new goods, the scope is more limited, a wholesaler or manufacturer will have a 'standard' price. However, *if* you find a good line and find yourself selling lots of them, go back to the supplier and negotiate: *I am now selling five of your gold bracelets per month and would like to buy a dozen, what price can you do?* If you are able, offering immediate payment helps your bargaining position. Don't enter the 'haggling' game until you know you decide how much you are prepared to buy, you will not be taken seriously if you negotiate a price for twelve gold bracelets then order six.

There is a thin line between 'Trade' and 'Public' - you may be a trader at an antiques fair specialising in porcelain but branching out into jewellery - you are a genuine trader even though you know less than an enthusiastic collector of jewellery. Or you may be a very knowledgeable collector who often sells a few items to raise cash to buy better items.

Every trade has its jargon, many 'public' buyers like to join in, in order to negotiate the best prices. In the last resort, traders recognise each other because they share the same idea of values and look for the same selling features. If you are eagerly trying to buy a bracelet, priced at £200.00 for £180.00 when the resale value in the trade is closer to £150.00, then the seller will be puzzled: either you are pretending to be a trader when you really have no idea as to the value, or he has misjudged the price. A man I met on a train boasted that he had negotiated a good price on an antique diamond ring, having nagged and pestered the seller until he brought the price down from £200.00 to £150.00. When he showed it to me I could see that he could easily have bought such a ring for under £100.00 by shopping around and paying the full asking price.

The following is a conversation between two traders at a trade market, antiques fair or secondhand shop, my translation is in brackets:

- WHAT CAN YOU DO ON THIS?   (How much are you asking?)
or
  WHAT'S YOUR TRADE ON THIS? (What is your Trade Price?)
or
  WHAT'S YOUR BEST TRADE?   (What is your best Trade Price?)
or
  WHAT'S YOUR BEST?   (What is your best price?)

- Thirty Five (£35.00)

A genuine trader will then examine the goods carefully for damage and to decide if he can make a profit.

- CAN YOU DO TWENTY EIGHT? (Will you accept £28.00?)

- THIRTY TWO IS MY VERY BEST (Best price is £32.00)

- IT'S VERY CLOSE, THIRTY ANY GOOD? (I can almost make a profit but really need to buy it at £30.00 for it to be worthwhile)

- OK
or
- NO, SORRY.

Don't forget to smile and say thank you.

Note the directness: there is no need to present a trade card, introduce yourself by name, or give a potted history of your experience in buying gold and silver - the seller only wants to know if a price can be agreed. Note too the politeness, you won't get very far shouting: 'GIVE YE A TENNER MATE??!' or feigning fright and proclaiming: 'HOW MUCH?!'

The above applies to bargaining for any secondhand or antique goods. Gold and silver have their own abbreviations:

- WHAT'S YOUR BEST ON THIS?

- THIRTEEN FIFTY (This could mean £13.50 or £1,350.00 If you are really a
                trader you   will know where the decimal point belongs)

- WHAT'S IT MADE OF? (Note, the buyer does not say 'Is it gold?' For
                £1,350.00 you would assume it was.   The
                question means: what carat gold is it?)

- EIGHTEEN (18ct gold)

- HALLMARKED?   (Is it hallmarked? If it is and you can't find the mark, the seller will show you where it is. Don't forget to take a good magnifier)

- NO, BUT IT'S BEEN TESTED

- DID YOU TEST IT YOURSELF? (This is a valid question)

- NO, BUT I DID BUY IT AS EIGHTEEN

- CAN I BRING IT BACK IF IT TURNS OUT NOT TO BE 18?

- OF COURSE!

Be suspicious if they say you can't bring the item back if it's misdescribed.[1] Don't forget to take the trader's card or stall number or telephone number in case there is a problem (if you have spent a lot of money they should offer you their card - they *want* you to come back next time). Test the item yourself when you get home, if it is not as described, telephone the seller to arrange to return it. If you turn up on the seller's doorstep two months later with your complaint, he will assume that you have had the item in stock for two months, couldn't sell it and are now looking for an excuse to return it.

Most traders are very honest, if your purchase turns out not to be as described you can return for a refund (or, more likely, a further discount). *However: you must be very clear as to what, exactly, you are buying.* If you say, 'Is it gold?' and the seller says, 'Yes', you cannot return the item on the basis that you *assumed* it was 18ct and it turned out to be 9ct.

---

[1] Be polite and be specific, eg. "If it turns out not to be 18ct can I bring it back?"
Do not be rude, eg. "If you're wrong and it's not genuine..."

AVOIDING BUYING STOLEN GOODS

Peter Hornsby in the *Antiques Trade Gazette* summed it up admirably:

There is a lot of coffee in Brazil. We know this, even if we cannot quantify the amount. Likewise, we are aware that there are masses of stolen goods circulating although we are unable to say precisely how many and how much they are worth.

When I worked in a shop in central London, buying scrap and jewellery, I knew, academically, that we were offered stolen goods. So I would insist on taking identification. The customer would write his name and address in our book, I would write the description of the goods and the price, and the customer would sign. I have watched many other people carry out the same procedure, yet few, it seems to me, actually check the customer's identification.

As a buyer it is *your* responsibility to check that the seller is genuine, a thief is not going to volunteer the information. If you buy something that is stolen it still belongs to the original owner even if it has passed through several hands, and the police will take it away to use in evidence at the trial. It is then up to you to sue the person you bought it from to try and reclaim your money, and you are unlikely to be successful.

I thought I was *so* good at following correct procedures until, one day, I found that life wasn't quite so simple.

I had two conversations on the telephone with the seller, I noted his name, copied down his phone number from caller display and kept an accurate record of the conversations. When he brought me the goods I very kindly helped fetch them from his car and made a mental note of the registration number, and just in case I mis-remembered, I also noted the time so that we could refer to the CCTV images. Inside the office I carefully checked that his identification was his own, copied down his home address onto a purchase slip, and he signed on the dotted line.

None of this helped. The goods were stolen, the police said that no such person lived at that address, there was nobody answering that phone number and they couldn't trace the car[1]. It was obvious that I had done my best[2] but, nevertheless, I got a severe telling-off. I should have taken

---

[1] I do suspect, that with all that information, the police *could* have traced the person but couldn't be bothered.

[2] The legal term for 'doing your best' is due diligence.

two forms of identification not one, and I should have taken photocopies.

One form of identification must include the seller's photograph or signature, the other must be a document no more than three months old that proves the address. For a list of documents see page 88.

When a customer shows you identification make sure that it is genuine. Does the signature match the document? Does the photograph match the face? Does their knowledge of an item they supposedly owned for ten years seem strangely scant?

If something doesn't seem 'right', keep chatting, keep alert, there will be clues. If the identification shows the seller to be Lieutenant Colonel Smythe-Edwards and he appears to be about eighteen years of age, you may wish to ask to him about his remarkable career. If someone shows you gold worth several thousand pounds and says, 'I won this in a raffle, is it worth anything?' you may wish to find out about the amazing raffle. If someone claims to live next to the hospital, ask them about the roadworks and the proposed shopping centre and the new wheelie bins. You will soon find out if they have someone else's identification.

Finally, when they show you their identification, take it from them and hold it in your hand while they fill in the purchase slip. You will be amazed at the number of sellers who suddenly don't know their own name and address!

A smile and a polite request 'to come back with some other identification' should be enough to send them away. Some of the more stupid sellers will persist, 'Oh no, this is not *my* identification, this is the identification of the old lady who's given me the goods to sell.'

On one occasion I politely turned away two children, explaining that I couldn't buy from children, but if their mummy had *really* sent them in, then she should write a letter. They returned a couple of hours later with a letter and I bought the goods. And another couple of hours later mummy arrived to complain that her darling little children had been forging letters and the goods were not for sale. After that, I would not buy from children, under any circumstances.

On another occasion we bought some medals from a middle aged man. The transaction involved considerable research, the seller called twice, his identification was in order. A couple of weeks later an older man called. He was the first man's father and claimed that the medals should not have been sold, they belonged to the family, they had been in the family for three generations and his son had no right to sell them. The dilemma: should we give the medals back? It slowly emerged that the son had inherited them from an uncle, so they were, legally, his property to sell. That the son didn't have his father's permission to sell them hardly seemed relevant to us. The moral: in cases of dispute, find out the facts before deciding what to do. If this case had been more obscure (eg. a dispute as to who had inherited the coins) then a court of law would have had to decide the outcome.

Another case in which the 'facts' turned out not to be what we expected involved the original owner spotting his stolen item in our shop window. He then did something very clever. He came in, said he wanted to buy it, left a deposit, got a receipt, then came back with the police. I looked up the purchase slip and was surprised to see I'd bought it from a regular dealer. The dealer was away on business when the police raided his house, but when he came back he told us the rest of the story. He had visited the seller in his house (he said you can always tell if it really is the person's home)...and when the police visited the address they found *lots* of stolen items.

You will note that in all the above cases, we did our best *(due diligence)* to ensure we weren't buying stolen property. If you simply buy anything without asking any questions or checking any identification, the police will assume you *knew* the items were stolen and *you* may end up in court.

All of the above is fine if you work from a shop or office or visit people in their homes. The situation at fairs, markets and boot sales is quite different. Imagine buying a gold ring from a stall at a boot sale and asking the seller for a written receipt - it's simply unheard of. Similarly, in Britain's fairs and markets, you see an item, you ask a price, you may haggle for a few seconds, then you produce cash. And if you ask for a receipt you will probably find that the seller hasn't got a receipt book and so scribbles something illegible on the back of a paper bag.

I, as a seller, will give a receipt if asked, but a fair or market is not like a shop, I can have a dozen people at the stall all at once, with dozens of hands touching my goods, and I don't like to stop serving customers just to write out a receipt. So if you are buying from a stall, offer to come back for the receipt when it's not too busy.

When I walk around the fairs as a buyer, I use my own system. I carry a sheet of paper with a form. The top of the page looks like this:

	Purchase Notes for secondhand items			
Name of antiques fair / market:			Date:	
Ref.	DESCRIPTION	Stand No. or vehicle reg	£ paid cash	Signature

I fill it in, the seller signs, it saves them from having to stop selling to find a receipt book and a pen.

The 'Ref' column is for your own use, assuming you have *some* form of stock control with stock numbers; include in the description any serial numbers or unique features. Inside stalls are numbered (the number probably won't be displayed, but the stallholder will know what it is). At an outside pitch use the vehicle registration number, this is the seller's 'identification'. The organiser *will* have a record of each seller's address and DVLA[1] *will* know the address of the registered owner of the vehicle.

I've been using this form for several years and only once has someone refused to sign.

REGISTRATION FOR DEALING IN SECONDHAND GOODS

Two areas (Kent[2] and North Yorkshire[3]) have introduced special schemes to monitor trade in secondhand goods, the intention being to combat trade in stolen goods. The unintended consequence is that every secondhand dealer, antiques dealer and fine art dealer has become caught up in the bureaucracy, no matter how legitimate they are.

The idea is simple. Traders register with the local council and keep a record of items bought, in an almost identical form to my own (see the previous page). This is their form, though you don't have to use this

---

[1] The central database for all vehicles in the U.K, the Driver and Vehicle Licensing Agency.

[2] See www.tradingstandards.gov.uk/kent/standard.htm

[3] See www.northyorks.gov.uk. The actual page, at time of going to press, is www.northyorks.gov.uk/index.aspx?articleid=2831

actual form providing you have a way of noting all the information. This is also a good 'template' to use as a general purchase note for your business.

Kent County Council Act 2001

Business Records

Product Reference

Page Number

Business Name

Seller's Name

Address

Post Code

The items listed below are my property. Duties and taxes have been paid on them. I have the full right to dispose of them. I understand that if I make a false declaration I could be liable to prosecution under the Fraud Act 2006

Signature

Full Description of Items

It is a legal requirement under the Kent County Council Act 2001, to record a sufficient description, where reasonably possible, to identify the article. This should include where appropriate, the number of items being sold, the type of material from which each article is made, the colour, artist's name, brand name or manufacture's identity if revealed by a symbol or mark on each article, the serial number(s), any distinguishing mark of feature on each article and any stock number or other information which is used to distinguish each article while in the dealer's possession. Failure to comply could lead to prosecution.

Date of Transaction and monies paid to the seller   £   :   p

Signature of Seller   Date   Time

ID Produced (record and identifiable serial numbers)

In accordance with the Kent County Council Act 2001 this record should be kept for a minimum of two years

There are several exemptions and many dozens of minor rules, though most of them don't apply to trading in gold and silver. Please remember that all of this only applies to dealing in secondhand goods in Kent and North Yorkshire.[1]

Extra Rules:

- when *selling* a watch for over £100.00 or any other item for over £500.00 you must note your *customer's* name and address
- if you are buying or selling at auction, you are buying from / selling to the auction house, not the actual owner / buyer of the goods

Exemptions (i.e. ignore the entire scheme) if:

- you will be re-selling an item for less than £10.00
- you very occasionally buy secondhand goods but don't resell them
- you take in secondhand goods only in part-exchange for new goods
- you are a pawnbroker
- you sell from a regular market
- you occasionally buy secondhand goods in Kent but don't sell in Kent
- you are a private individual (eg. selling your collection)

Final Rule:

- all the rules apply if you sell in Kent, even if you buy the goods all over the country

INTERNET AUCTIONS AND ONLINE SHOPS

For most people 'internet auction' means eBay, though the trend, in the last couple of years, has been towards getting customers to list items in mini-shops (eBay Shops) in addition to selling by auction. But eBay is not the only one. A major competitor (for non-auction selling) is Amazon. You create a list of products, pay to keep each one on the list for a few weeks or months, if it sells you also pay commission, if it doesn't sell you've only lost the small listing fee.

---

[1] Although there's a huge amount of information about the Kent Act (Kent County Council Act 2001), there is minimal information about the North Yorkshire Act. I do know that North Yorkshire 'copied' Kent, so I assume the rules are the same. The only additional rule I found was that, in North Yorkshire, it is an offence to buy an item for more than £10.00 from a child aged under 16.

Each item *will* take you 45mns to an hour to create. So if you spend several hours creating listings for low-value products that you probably won't sell...it's not very exciting. If, on the other hand, you already have a database of products (on your accounts system or an existing website) and you spend a couple of hours transferring them to your new 'shop', you may end up with hundreds of products listed and, hopefully, you will sell a few each day. I don't have experience of selling in this way but I do have experience of eBay in its traditional sense: selling by internet auction.

As a hobby, and if you forget the fact that eBay is about the most complicated computer-based system in existence, and that you will spend hundreds of hours on the computer and will sometimes make a profit and sometimes make a loss – go for it! If you intend to use eBay for part of your living, then regard it as 'iffy because it is very time-consuming.

In theory you can list and sell an item for as little as 50 minutes' work but in practice you should allow an average of an hour per item. The following are my timings, so when someone says, "It only takes five minutes to list an item on eBay!" ask them if they've allowed for the following:

Take one photograph,   5mns
If the item is valuable, take a few more   5mns
Crop and enhance them on the computer   5mns
(professional photographers will view these timings with amazement, they will spend a few hours on each photograph)
Measure, weigh, test, look up hallmarks   5mns
Write some text   5mns
Re-write it, check it, get a friend to check it   5mns
(a one line, *Hallmarked 9ct bracelet, 21g* will take 1mn, but some research will take an hour, on average it *will* take you more than 15mns)
List it on eBay   5mns
(but only if it's *very* simple and you have already spent considerable time setting up templates, not if you have to think about what to type into each box or what to select from each option)
During the auction bidders will email questions   5mns
(a rare item can attract a dozen questions involving an hour of extra research)
Processing the payment   5mns
(*far* longer if you actually keep accounts and need to reconcile your bank account and PayPal account)
Packing and posting   5mns
(this assumes you don't count the time actually going to the Post Office)

Total   **50mns**

So is all this time worthwhile if you are using eBay for part of your living? Sometimes. It depends on whether you are listing one-offs or multiple items; whether they are standard modern items or rare collector's items; whether they are low-value or high-value.

For one-off low-value items do not spend the time, you will end up working for between £1.00 and £2.00 per hour[1].

If you have several of an item, use a 'listing system' such as Turbo Lister (eBay charge a monthly fee for their 'pro' version). So if you have ten *different* items but have fifty of each, it might involve ten hours of work but you will end up with 500 items that will automatically 'feed' themselves onto eBay.[2] Then, hopefully, you will sell a few each day.

Another way in which eBay works well is if you have a rare collector's item. An 18th century silver hallmarked tankard in good condition *is* saleable, but you won't necessarily get the best price in your local auction, local antiques fair or local shop. On eBay collector's from all around the world will see it, and if it really is desirable you *will* get dozens of bids. This doesn't mean that you will make a profit if you paid a lot for it to start with, but providing you have a low reserve price it *will sell*.

Do keep a very close eye on the charges. The listing charges aren't huge but they add up. The commission is high compared with other methods of selling (especially when you add PayPal's commission) but not frighteningly so. However, when you add into the equation the fact that many of your items won't sell, you must assume that the 'real' cost of charges on eBay is between 20% and 30%.

Finally, a warning about high-value transactions. If you are paid by PayPal (and nearly everyone will pay by PayPal) the money is not guaranteed. If, for any reason whatsoever, the buyer complains, PayPal will refund the money and take it back from your bank account.[3] This can happen because the item got lost in the post (through no fault of your own) or the buyer decides he doesn't like the item and claims it's not as described or he doesn't like the condition and claims that it arrived damaged.

---

[1] This doesn't apply if you are selling your own possessions (with no 'profit' to be made) and treat the time spent purely as 'enjoyment'.

[2] There are various ways of doing this: one every few days or weeks, or list one each time the previous one sells and / or re-list any that don't sell.

[3] When you sign up to PayPal you give them your bank details and permission to reclaim any money they wish, there is no choice about this.

CREATING (AND SELLING FROM) A WEBSITE

To create a website merely to have a 'presence' on the internet, any number of ISPs (Internet Service Providers) will give you free space along with your email address. The disadvantage is that you will have a complicated web address, e.g. instead of www.mydomain.co.uk it might be www.btinternet.com/mydomain/home.

To create a website that is a serious part of a business you must first buy a domain name (there are many online sellers, search the internet for *domain name registration*), the price can be as low as £10.00, rising to hundreds of pounds for extra space and other services such as mailboxes, databases and webstats.

A website can list products and give information only (customers must email or telephone to find out how to buy products), or it can also take money online. The software to create the former might cost a couple of hundred pounds, the software for the latter, several hundred pounds. If you want the same software to track orders from your supplier to your stock room to your picking and packing departments, you will need to budget a few thousand pounds.

If you love computers and are prepared to spend lots of time learning, there are free programs, but they *will* be very complicated to use and there will be no support if they go wrong. If you have no aptitude for, or patience with, computers whatsoever, there is always the option of getting someone else to design and maintain the website, and computer-literate staff can process orders.

The design, maintenance and marketing of websites is an entire industry; mail order and fulfilment is another vast industry. I am not a specialist and nobody can summarise the workings of two multi-billion pound industries in a few paragraphs, but hopefully the above will point you in the right direction.

For general advice about creating a website see page 82.

TAKING MONEY (PAYMENT METHODS)

Credit Cards[1]

Credit cards are accepted in all retail jewellers, nearly all up-market antiques shops, and some up-market antiques fairs and antiques centres. Most stallholders at antiques fairs and owners of small secondhand / junk shops do not accept cards. If you decide you need to take cards to sell by mail[2] (they call it MOTO, Mail Order / Telephone Order) then, at the same time, ask the bank about taking cards in person.

To take credit cards you need to open a 'Merchant Account' for taking credit card money[3]. If you are going to take cards online you also need a Payment Service Provider (PSP). Some PSPs are owned by banks, some belong to software companies. Finally you need a 'gateway' between the card system and the products on your website. If you don't have a website you won't need a PSP but you'll still need a 'gateway' in the form of a terminal (some plug into the phone line, some are wireless) or a 'virtual terminal' (you operate it online).

Each of these will cost you money. Your bank will charge a monthly fee for operating the account, the PSP will charge you a monthly fee *and* a percentage of the money you take. In addition, you are well-advised to pay a monthly fee for a 'service contract' to sort out problems with the actual website. Even if you don't have a website and go straight for a Merchant Account with a main bank, they will charge you rental for the terminal or a monthly charge for the online ('virtual') terminal.

You can shortcut this system by spending several hundred pounds on software that will let you design and run a website with built-in e-commerce, and where the software company *is* the PSP *and* they handle the account with the acquiring bank *and* give software support. Of course, the monthly fee and / or commission will be high because they are supplying all the services as one package.

If you think this all sounds expensive, it is.

---

[1] Throughout this section I refer to 'credit cards'. I mean this to include debit cards. The one card that doesn't fit into the category of 'credit cards and debit cards' is American Express, which requires a separate Merchant Account.

[2] There is a list of suppliers on page 179

[3] Ultimately, all credit card money is moved about by a handful of 'Acquiring Banks', Alliance Leicester, American Express, Bank of Scotland, Barclaycard, HSBC, Lloyds, Royal Bank of Scotland with NatWest, and Ulster Bank.

There is another type of PSP (a *Bureau* PSP) which is aimed at the smaller business and the individual. Their selling feature is that they are simple to operate. Their commission will be high (between 4.5% and 8%) but there will be no monthly charge and no need to open a special bank account. Examples are PayPal and Nochex.

For your customers buying online this means they are given the payment options for your Bureau PSP (eg *Paypal* or *Nochex)* but not the option *Pay by Credit Card.* The customer *can* pay from their card (they will pay PayPal or Nochex who then pass the money to you) or they can open a PayPal or Nochex account then pay directly from the account.[1]

PayPal is linked to eBay (in fact, it is owned by eBay) and a PayPal account, eBay account and website *can* all be connected (it's never as simple as they imply, but it can be done). An advantage of PayPal is that customers from around the world can pay in their local currency and it arrives in your PayPal account in your currency. A disadvantage is that it is expensive and has hundreds of rules. Details: www.paypal.co.uk [2]

Nochex is British and is far simpler than PayPal. As with PayPal it can be connected to websites, The disadvantage is that it operates only in the U.K and so you cannot accept money from overseas. Details: www.nochex.co.uk.

For a list of several PSPs (of all types) see page 180.

Just like cheques, credit cards can 'bounce' (they call it *chargeback* or *reversal*) but unlike cheques this can happen up to six months after the transaction, and the agreement you signed *will* give the bank / PSP permission to reclaim the money from your bank account. PayPal boasts a Seller *Protection Policy* to protect you against this, but if you study their terms and conditions you will find that many transactions are excluded from the scheme (*ineligible*) and you cannot simply accept *eligible* transactions, you must accept all transactions then enter into long arguments with customers whose money isn't guaranteed...and that's the reason I discontinued PayPal.

---

[1] If you say to yourself, "It doesn't sound so simple for the customer" you have a good point, many find these services over-complicated, especially if they think they must open an account with the PSP.

[2] If you are in the UK use .co.uk rather than .com

Bank Accounts

Next, we have a somewhat obvious solution that is overlooked by many traders. An ordinary high street bank account....and not just for cheques.

Customers can transfer money directly into an account. All banks now give customers access to their bank accounts online, so for those who actually use the system it *is* very easy. They *do* have to enter your sort code and account number the first time, but then they can 'save' the details so that future transfers are easy, *far* quicker than paying by credit card. Alternatively, banks offer telephone banking.

The following banks operate the *Faster Payments* system, the money will arrive within two hours of being transferred:

Bank	Availability	Value Limit
Alliance & Leicester	Phone and internet	£250
Bank of Scotland	Phone and internet	Retail customers- £2,500 Corporate customers £10,000
Barclays	Phone and internet	£10,000
Citibank	Only available to corporate customers via Internet	£10,000
Clydesdale (including Yorkshire Bank)	Phone and internet	£500
Co-operative	Phone and internet	£1000
Northern Bank (Danske)	Phone and internet	£10,000
HSBC	Yes	Personal internet banking £5,000 All other channels £10,000
Lloyds TSB	Phone and internet	Retail customers £10,000 Corporate customers £10,000
Nationwide	Yes, phone and internet	£1,000
Northern Rock	Customers with saving accounts, via the internet	N/A
Royal Bank of Scotland (including Natwest & Ulster Bank)	Phone and internet	£10,000

List updated April 2010, source: www.chapsco.co.uk/faster_payments

The only disadvantage with an ordinary bank account is that it's only an ordinary bank account. When a customer transfers money there is no 'internet payment system' to tell you who they are or what the money is for. They must email or telephone to tell you.

Another method is so stunningly simple that most people wouldn't think of it. Get someone to pay cash into your bank account. We have one customer who regularly telephones at 1pm to say that he's going to lunch and will be back in twenty minutes and please can he place an order. I take the order, he goes to lunch, while he is out he pops into a branch of the bank, fills in a paying-in slip and pays cash. By the time he gets back to the office he has an email from us telling him when the goods will be posted.

These methods are not restricted to this country or to our currency. Any bank will gladly let you open a US Dollar or Euro account (because they charge a monthly fee) and then you can accept bank transfers from overseas.

Other payment systems

There are three payment methods that do not require any recourse to computers.

Western Union is a method of transferring cash from one part of the world to another, the buyer pays cash at a *Western Union* outlet, the seller goes to HIS local *Western Union* (usually a corner shop) with identification and they hand over the cash.

One tip: check that there *is* a convenient Western Union outlet near you. The one time I accepted a Western Union payment I had to visit eight outlets before finding one that was open, had a working computer, had someone who knew how to operate the computer, had someone who had authority to pay the money and actually had cash on the premises.

Cash is always an option. Make sure it's sent by Recorded Delivery (for small amounts) or Special Delivery (for large amounts). Some owners of 'cash businesses' like this, they take cash, they don't like to hold cash on the premises, they post it to their supplier, they save on bank charges, the supplier saves on credit card commission.

Finally, an intriguing service in the UK that enables you to accept cheques in Dollars or Euros - you physically post your cheques to a company and they post back (or transfer into your bank account) a cheque in Pounds Sterling. The cost is £1.00 per transaction plus the cost of postage (I recommend Recorded Delivery). The only disadvantage is that you get a poor exchange rate.   Details: www.auctionchex.com

BUYING AND SELLING BULLION

When selling bullion (coins or bars) it may be necessary to compare prices within the hour. One man offered us a hundred gold coins and we quoted a price. He spent the morning comparing prices and came back three hours later. We looked at our screen - prices had fallen by 50p per coin. Profit margins on bullion vary between 1½% and 5%[1] which means that a bullion dealer may need that extra 50p per coin to make the transaction worthwhile. A good tip: ask each bullion dealer his buying and selling price. Tell him the quantity involved but do not tell him whether you are buying or selling. The bullion dealer must then quote a keen price. Some people 'play' with gold investments and if they hear the price is volatile they may buy in the morning and sell in the afternoon; or sell in the morning and buy in the afternoon depending which way they think the price is moving. Nobody knows which way the price of gold will move: people who tap their nose and say they have been told on good authority that the price will rise (or fall) are deluded.

Getting quotes on bullion is similar to getting quotes for hamburgers: it is fast. Write the prices down or you will forget, especially when telephoning or calling at several dealers and receiving dozens of similar prices. Bullion dealers have no patience with customers who ask more for their coins than the dealer's own selling price and can even become frustrated by the small customer who spends several minutes over just one coin - it is the 'telephone dealing' involving hundreds of coins which interests bullion dealers. On the other hand, there are times when the gold price is depressed the bullion dealer isn't doing much business and so even if you are only buying a few coins he might have time to chat and show you several (or even several dozen) coins to choose from.

The scenario at a jewellery shop is very different. The shopkeeper should give advice, telephone the bullion dealer for the best price and may even be able to show you a few coins to choose from. For his efforts the jeweller will expect to make a profit on the price from the bullion dealer. Most jewellers cannot be bothered with gold coins at all.

If you prefer to buy bars rather than coins, you will be offered (from a bullion dealer) bars with the emblem of the Swiss bank Credit Suisse or the Spanish bank Semsa. You will not be offered (or want to buy) unmarked 'lumps' of gold, because you would have no way of knowing

---

[1] For just one or two coins allow an extra 5% at a bullion dealer. I doubt that a jewellers shop would be bothered for less than 10% or 15% profit.

what it was made of. Bars can come in any size from 1g to 1Kg. Although it might seem 'romantic' to own a gold bar, coins are better. Everyone recognises the designs on, and weights of, coins. A forged coin would be easy to spot (and there would be no point in making the 'forgery' of the correct carat gold, it would be worth the same as the genuine coin). Bars, by contrast, are more difficult to recognise. You may come to sell it in a few years and the buyer is unsure of its content and wants to melt and assay it. So it's better to stick to coins.

Things do change. In Germany[1] it is possible to buy gold from a vending machine, either as 1g bars or as small coins (up to about 3g). The price is electronically updated every fifteen minutes. But the amounts (and values) are relatively small and you pay a high price relative to the gold value.

Confirmation of a deal (whether buying or selling) is a legally binding contract and *is* enforced in the bullion trade. If you agree, for instance, to sell ten sovereigns and then change your mind, the bullion dealer will make a note of your name and will not deal with you again. If you back out of a few deals, word will spread and nobody will deal with you. The same rule applies to bullion dealers themselves, if he orders a hundred sovereigns for you and then you decide not to buy, the bullion dealer still has to pay for them and may have to resell them at a loss. It is for this reason that you may be asked for a deposit which will cover any losses should you back out of the deal when buying, or you may have to call in person to sell coins. Alternatively, you could post coins to the bullion dealer or bank and accept the price prevailing on the day.

---

[1] By the time you read this the system may have become popular in other countries, or it may have been abandoned altogether. .

TAX

There are no special VAT[1] rules concerning gold and silver for private (non-trade) buyers or for trade buyers who are not VAT-registered. It's just the same as any other standard-rated VAT item, if you buy from a VAT-registered trader, you pay VAT.

If you visit a country outside the European Union and bring back goods valued at more than £390.00[2] you must declare them (by going through the RED channel at the port or airport). You will then be charged VAT. This applies to a 'traveller' with items 'for private use'. If the items are of uncertain value (eg. gold bars) Revenue & Customs will confiscate them for assay and give them back when the value is known and the VAT paid. It is not illegal to import gold, there are no restrictions in this country, so don't feel shy about declaring it. Of course, if you *don't* want to pay the VAT, then don't declare it – this is known as smuggling.[3]

The above applies to private individuals with items for private use. If you are a trader you will declare everything you import.

If a VAT-registered trader walks into a bullion dealer to sell coins (or bars) he will charge VAT and will normally provide a VAT invoice and get paid the net amount plus the VAT. That is OK if the bullion dealer has checked that the trader really is registered for VAT but if the bullion dealer *hasn't* verified the trader's identity and VAT number, he will not pay him the VAT, he will pay only the net amount and pay the VAT directly to Revenue & Customs. This is to prevent fraud.[4]

Income tax is payable on all income over a certain amount though there are many allowances, see www.hmrc.gov.uk or ask an accountant for details. The important word here is 'income', you are not exempt because you bought the item thirty years ago or because you inherited it or because you only deal in cash.

Whether 'dabbling' in buying and selling along with a full time-job or buying and selling as your only source of income, it is wise to keep a

---

[1] This is Value Added Tax, known in the USA as Sales Tax

[2] As of 2010, but you may wish to check this, thresholds change over the years.

[3] I feel obliged to point out to Revenue & Customs that this is intended as a warning not an instruction

[4] Pretend traders would 'invent' a VAT number, sell scrap with a VAT invoice (charging VAT) then disappear before Revenue & Customs could find them, the 17.5% VAT being, for them, extra profit, on top of their 4% or 5% margin. And so much money was involved, Revenue & Customs were losing millions of pounds per month, with new scammers setting up and disappearing on a daily basis.

record of all money spent and received. If you pass all 'business' money through a separate bank account, it will then be easy to approach an accountant at a later date should you need advice about income tax.

If your sole venture into the world of buying and selling gold and silver constitutes selling unwanted jewellery for one tenth of what it originally cost, then you may prefer to keep quiet about your new income. The tax man probably does not have the resources to follow up the thousands of people who, each summer weekend, rent a stall at a boot sale and sell their own personal junk and jewellery, he will be more interested in those who use boot sales to bring in a steady undeclared income. If you are worried about the tax man, keep a record of how much the jewellery cost and how much you sold it for so that you can prove that you are not really running an undeclared multi-million pound business.

Bullion bought from companies outside the EU (including the Channel Islands) is not liable for Value Added Tax *provided* the bullion remains abroad. The moment it is brought into the country VAT must be paid.

For VAT-registered traders a special scheme operates to protect Britain's art treasures, and the scheme includes all secondhand goods. Instead of having to charge VAT on the entire sale, VAT is only payable on the profit. Keep a record of all secondhand purchases (details of who you bought them from[1]) and all secondhand sales (usually just the amount[2]), deduct one from the other, VAT is only payable on the difference.

When someone dies their wealth (*estate*) will be subject to inheritance tax if it exceeds the tax-free band. Valuables made of gold and silver will comprise part of the estate and so have to be valued. The valuation will also be helpful for future reference should capital gains tax be due.

Capital Gains Tax is only payable on the gain, i.e. the difference between the value when acquired and the value when disposed. 'Disposed' doesn't just mean selling the item, it also means giving it away as a gift, transferring it to someone else, exchanging it for something else or receiving compensation for it (eg an insurance claim). The tax applies to possessions worth more than £6000.00, and 'possessions' include art, antiques and collectables (including coins, whether purely collectable, purely bullion, or anywhere in between) but *not* bullion bars. For a *summary* of the rules (and the latest rate) see www.hmrc.gov.uk, but please do see an accountant to find out how this tax might affect you.

---

[1] Devise yourself a form similar to that on page 116

[2] For items sold for over £500.00 you must also record the name and address of your customer

FUTURES TRADING, GOLD LEASING AND PRICE FLUCTUATIONS

When spending large amounts of money (several thousand pounds per transaction) a commodity broker may be used for giving advice on when to buy and sell. In this way gold is bought and sold not on the price of the moment ('spot' price) but on the anticipated price of months ahead.

A seller of gold might promise to supply and will agree a selling price yet will not be able to deliver the gold for at least a month or two. No gold has changed hands, only an agreement (a 'contract') to sell gold at an agreed 'future' price has been entered into. The seller is gambling on the price falling so that when the time comes to sell the gold at the agreed price (gold which he hasn't physically got) he may physically buy it at the new lower price, thus making a profit.

Conversely, a contract may be taken out to *buy* gold at an agreed future price. The gamble here is that the price of gold will rise so that the gold (bought 'on paper' at a relatively low price) can then be sold at the new higher price. In practice, it is not necessary to turn the paper transactions into physical gold nor is it necessary to wait months before closing the deal. Contracts can be terminated at any time and the resulting profit or loss calculated.

Each instruction you telephone through to a broker is tape recorded so that there is no misunderstanding as to whether you meant 'buy' or 'sell'. Each contract must, of course, be backed by wealth to the value of the potential losses - commodity brokers are very strict about this, so that if it all goes wrong and you end up owing lots of money, you still have something to sell, eg. your home.

It is as if the futures market was devised by a time traveller buying and selling gold in different time zones simultaneously, each time zone's price rising and falling by the minute - usually in line with each other but at varying speeds - and managing to balance his books. The arithmetic is complicated, it is even possible to take out contracts so that you make money whether the price rises *or* falls; but in this case you will lose money if the price is the same when the contract matures. Decisions to buy and sell are further complicated by the unpredictable nature of the gold price. Sometimes international political tension, interest rates or currency strengths affect the price of gold. Often the price of gold is more influenced more by thousands of confused speculators buying or selling Futures at the same time.

Price fluctuations have become even more volatile with the advent of the latest computer technology: instead of predicting prices on the basis of supply and demand, the latest computer programmes predict the pattern of buying and selling *caused* by a price change and then instruct other computers to put in orders to buy or sell. A BBC *From Our Own Correspondent* talk summed the situation up nicely: once, he said, when the sea froze over, ships couldn't sail and this affected the local currency markets; but today, he continued, there is so much speculation with international traders 'buying' and 'selling' all currencies, that the actual physical situation has very little effect. Exactly the same is true of gold, the ultimate 'currency'.

If you are a jeweller who has physical gold in store and would like to 'invest' it as if it were money; or if you are a bullion dealer promising to supply gold to clients on a particular date, then Futures dealing is a good idea - you possess the actual gold you are dealing in. If you are dealing in commodities simply as a gamble then your broker may advise you to buy gold one day, orange juice another and live hogs the next. Your security in these cases is not your stock of gold and if prices turn against you overnight you could wake up in the morning to phone calls from your bank manager or commodity broker claiming your home. Be warned: this has happened. It is all too easy for the 'casual investor' to become an addicted gambler and spend day and night watching a computer screen to see if he is making or losing money.

A variation on this theme is to guarantee your wealth against a bank loan (as is normal) but to use gold as collateral. The scheme is known as 'gold leasing' and is a service provided to jewellers by bullion banks. There are various schemes. The loan can be secured against any suitable wealth and paid in the form of gold which is then used in manufacture; or a jeweller's stock of gold can be used as security to borrow gold, but the actual payment made in pounds sterling. Either way, when the arithmetic is completed, the effect is that of a cheap loan.

The situation with silver is quite different. Whereas gold is mostly stored (hoarded) or made into jewellery, its industrial uses being few, silver *is* used in large quantities in industry. Another factor is that the mining of silver is also quite different from that of gold. Silver is a by-product of mining lead, zinc, copper and gold, and so is regarded as a 'bonus' - the mines will continue to produce silver even if the price is low. So if demand falls and the mines keep producing silver the result is a glut of silver on the world market and this can cause a lack of confidence and a sudden fall in the price. The silver price is more volatile than the price of gold.

PART THREE: USEFUL INFORMATION AND FASCINATING FACTS

FOREIGN DATES [1]

Our dating system, starting with zero for the birth of Jesus, only applies to 'Christian' countries. Other countries use different systems. **ARAB COUNTRIES** started numbering AH (after Hegira, the flight of Mohammed from Mecca to Medina in 622 AD) and used the lunar year of 354 days instead of 365 days. So the simplest way to calculate a date is to say: their year is about 3% shorter than ours, so deduct 3% then add 622. **SIAM** [Thailand] used three dating systems: the 'Buddhist' era (BE) starting 543 BC (deduct 543 from the date); the 'Bangkok / Ratanakosinel-sok' (RS) era starting 1781 (add 1781 to the date); the 'Chula-Sakarat' (CS) era starting 638 AD (add 638 to the date). **INDIA** has two main eras, 'Saka' from part of Northern India starting 78 AD (add 78 to the date); 'Vikrama / Samvat' starting 57 BC (subtract 57 from the date). **CHINA** has no easy way of calculating dates were based on a sixty year cycle.

	1	2	3	4	5	6	7	8	9	0	10	100	1000
ARABIC-TURKISH	١	٢	٣	٤	٥	٦	٧	٨	٩	•	١٠	١••	١•••
MALAY PERSIAN	١	٢	٣	٤	٥	٦	٧	٨	٩	•			
CHINESE, JAPANESE, KOREAN, ANNAMESE (Ordinary)	一	二	三	四	五	六	七	八	九		十	百	千
CHINESE, JAPANESE, KOREAN, ANNAMESE (Official)	壹	貳	叄	肆	伍	陸	柒	捌	玖		拾	(半=½)	
INDIAN	९	२	३	४	५	६	७	८	९	०			
SIAMESE	๑	๒	๓	๔	๕	๖	๗	๘	๙	๐	๑๐	๑๐๐	
BURMESE	၁	၂	၃	၄	၅	၆	၇	၈	၉	၀			

FOREIGN NAMES ON COINS

DEUTSCHES or DEUTSCHLAND	GERMANY
EIRE	REPUBLIC OF IRELAND
HELVETICA	SWITZERLAND
MALAGASY	MADAGASCAR
NORGES	NORWAY
SUOMEN TRASAVALTA	FINLAND
SVERIGE	SWEDEN

German Democratic Republic was East Germany, Federal Republic of Germany was West Germany

---

[1] This is a summary of an un-signed article from COIN YEAR BOOK 1981.

THE PRE-DECIMAL SYSTEM OF COINAGE

Gold coins

The specification of gold coins has remained unchanged since 1820, they were made of 22ct gold (916.66 parts per thousand) the remaining metal (83.33 parts per thousand) being copper. There was a five pound coin of 39.94g. (diameter 36.02mm); £2.00 coin 15.9761g (diameter 28.4mm); £1.00 coin (Sovereign) 7.9881g (diameter 22.05mm); £0.50 (Half Sovereign) 3.9940g (diameter 19.30mm).

Silver coins

Before 1920 (i.e. up to and including 1919) these were made of 925 parts per thousand silver; before 1947 (i.e. up to and including 1946) 500 parts per thousand. From 1947 'silver' coins contain no silver but comprise cupro-nickel - 75% copper and 25% nickel.

Copper and brass coins

Brass 3d: 79% copper, 1% nickel, 20% zinc
1d, ½d and ¼d: Pre-1923 95% copper, 4% tin, 1% zinc
                1923-1942 95½% copper, 3% tin, 1½% zinc
                from 1942 97% copper, ½% tin, 2½% zinc

A wealth of information can be found cunningly hidden in the Royal Mint website at www.royalmint.com/Corporate/facts/circulation.aspx. If this location has moved, have a hunt around www.royalmint.com.

Britain changed to decimal coinage on 15th February 1971. By 1971 the halfpenny was worth so little that even the banks excluded it from calculations and brass threepences were collected by children as curios. The new halfpenny was demonetised in 1984; the one pound coin was introduced in 1983, the one pound note was withdrawn in 1988 and the £2.00 coin was introduced in 1998. I now find that the elderly have great delight in explaining the old coin system to me - incorrectly; while schoolchildren explain the old coin system to me correctly, having learnt about it at school. To solve many a family dispute, here are the facts:

12 Pennies (d) = 1 Shilling (s or /-)
20 shillings = 1 Pound (£)

There were in £1.00:			Conversions to decimal (to the nearest £0.001p)
¼d	X	960	¼d = £0.001
½d	X	480	½d = £0.002
1d	X	240	1d = £0.004
3d	X	80	3d = £0.125
6d	X	40	6d = £0.025
1/-	X	20	1/- = £0.05
2/-	X	10	2/- = £0.10
2/6	X	8	2/6 = £0.125
4/-	X	5	4/- = £0.20
5/-	X	4	5/- = £0.25
10/-	X	2	10/- = £0.50

The last pre-decimal coins

¼d Last issue 1956. Common name, farthing

½d Last issue 1967 Halfpenny ('Hay-penny')

1d Last issue 1967 Penny

3d Last issue 1967 Silver to 1941 (1944 in the colonies) Brass from 1937 to 1967. Slang name, Joey

6d Last issue 1967 2 X 6d = 5p. Slang name, Tanner

1/- Last issue 1966 Still in circulation as 5p coins Slang name, Bob

2/- Last issue 1967 Still in circulation as 10p coins Common name, Florin or Two Shilling

2/6 Last issue 1967 Common names Half Crown, or Two and Six.

4/- Issued as a circulation coin 1887 to 1890 (This was intended as a prelude to decimalisation)

5/- Last issue as a circulation coin 1902; issued as a commemorative coin from 1910 (500 silver); cupro-nickel from 1951. Common name, Crown; slang name, Dollar

10/- Last issue 1967 A bank note not a coin.

COUNTING PRE-DECIMAL COINS BY WEIGHT

When counting British silver coins, any combination of silver coins will weigh 110.5g per £1.00 face value.

RARE COIN DATES

The following dates are worth looking up in a coin catalogue but, beware, the catalogue price ('book price') is not necessarily the price you will get, you must phone a coin dealer to get a realistic price. The letter after each date refers to the minimum condition the coin must be, to be of value:

F = FINE, VF = VERY FINE, EF = EXTRA FINE

Illustrations of each grade can be found at the front of any coin catalogue. A *proof* coin is made from a special blank polished to a mirror finish and presented in a box for collectors - the slightest finger mark on one of these will ruin its value as a proof coin. The grade of a coin is objective - it is not relative to its age. Thus, a coin which is grade VF (Very Fine) is of that grade irrespective of its age - there is no such grade as 'slightly worn but very good for its age'.

FARTHINGS ¼d.	HALFPENNIES ½d.	PENNIES
1685 TO 1692 F	1685 TO 1692 (tin)£F	1797 F
1714£ F	1825 F	1827£F
1717 F	1845 F	1843£F
1771 F	1865/3* F	1849£F
1844 F		
1863 F	**TWOPENCE 2d.**	
1874*£F	1797 F	

BRASS 3d.	SILVER 3d.	GROAT 4d.	SIXPENCES 6d.
1939 VF	1868* F	1847/6* F	1821*£F
1946 F	1893* F	1851 F	1854 F
1949 F	1906 F	1852 F	1878* F
1950 F			1923 F

SHILLINGS 1/-	FLORINS 2/-	HALF CROWNS 2/6	CROWNS 2/6
1818 F	Gothic F	1823* F	1847 Gothic£F
1848*F	1905 F	1841£ F	1893 'LVII' F
1851 F	1913 F	1843 F	1898 'LXXI' F
1854£F	1925 F	1848£ F	1902 F
1862 F	1932 F	1902 VF	1902 Proof£
1863 F		1903£ F	1928-30 F
1889*F		1905£ F	1936£ F
1905*F		1930 VF	1937* Proof£
		1953 EF	1951* Proof£

KEY

* Only certain rare varieties of these dates are of value - see a coin catalogue.
£ Listed in coin catalogues at over £20.00

BETTER-THAN-GOLD BULLION COINS

Bullion coins are coins which are bought and sold on a value-for-weight basis. This price changes at least once a day with the changing price of gold. In Britain the common bullion coins are the Sovereign (one pound coin: 1/4oz of 22ct gold) and the half Sovereign (½ pound coin: 1/8th oz of 22ct gold). Also popular is the Krugerrand (contains 1oz of pure gold).

If a coin is polished or damaged in any way it will become worthless as a collector's coin. Avoid coins which have been mounted as jewellery or polished or which have solder marks where loops or mounts have been removed or which are damaged by scratches, dents around the edge (edge knocks) or which have holes or even holes which have been filled in (plugged). If a coin has been worn as jewellery for even a short time it will become polished as it rubs against clothes and skin.

The dates listed below are *sometimes* worth more than bullion value providing they are not polished or damaged *and providing they are in at least EF condition.* But not always. If the bullion price of a sovereign was £80.00 and a rare date would sell to a collector for £150.00...but then the gold price rose and the bullion value became £180.00, there will no longer be any additional collector's value

SOVEREIGNS	HALF SOVEREIGNS	NOTES
1879	George III: all*	* Very rare
1908c**	George IV : all*	** Extremely rare
1913c**	William IV: all*	
1916c**		Letters refer to the mint mark
1917**	1850	which can be found just
1919m	1877m	above the date. No mint
1920m**	1881m	mark indicates that the coin
1920s**	1882m	was minted in London.
1921m**	1884m	
1921s**	1885m	There were no sovereigns
1922m**	1886m	minted between 1933 and
1922s**	1887m	1956 and between 1969 and
1923m*	1881s*	1973 (except for the 1937
1923s*	1882s*	proof sovereign) and there
1924s**	1904p	were no half sovereigns
1924sa**	1908p	minted between 1926 and
1926s	1909p	1979 (except for the 1937
1927m**	1918p	proof sovereign).
1928m*	1926s**	
1929m		
1930m		
1931m		

WEIGHTS AND PURITIES CHARTS

The charts on the following pages show the precious metal content of gold and silver coins and medallions. The purities are given in parts per thousand; the weight (of *pure* gold / silver) is given in grams.

Coins

Most gold coins are of a high purity, mostly 900 parts per thousand in Europe, always 916 parts per thousand in Britain. The chart gives the information needed to check the weight and calculate the value. To find the purity calculate ACTUAL GOLD VALUE ÷ GROSS WEIGHT (Don't forget to convert the ounces to grams: 1 oz = 31.1035 grams).

British silver-coloured coins were made of 925 parts per thousand silver up to 1919 and 500 parts per thousand silver from 1920 to 1946. Most other countries changed the purity and size of their coins several times.

Gold Coins

COUNTRY	DENOMINATION	GROSS WEIGHT (g.)	ACTUAL GOLD VALUE (oz)	NOTES
AUSTRIA	1 DUCAT	3.49	0.1107	1 DUCAT AND 5
	4 DUCAT	13.97	0.4430	DUCAT COINS
	10 CORONA	3.34	0.0980	DATED 1915 ARE
	20 CORONA	6.78	0.1960	ALMOST CERTAINLY
	100 CORONA	33.88	0.9802	RESTRIKES
BELGIUM	10 FRANCS	3.23	0.0933	IN PROPORTION:
	20 FRANCS	6.45	0.1867	25FR. 40FR.
				100FR.
CANADA	5 DOLLARS	8.36	0.2419	
	10 DOLLARS	16.72	0.4838	
	20 DOLLARS	18.28	0.5287	
FRANCE	5 FRANCS	1.61	0.0467	IN PROPORTION:
	10 FRANCS	3.23	0.0933	50FR. 50FR. 100F
	20 FRANCS	6.46	0.1867	EXCEPTION:
				100FR. 1929-36
				=6.55g/0.1895oz
GERMANY	5 MARKS	1.99	0.0576	
	10 MARKS	3.99	0.1152	
	20 MARKS	7.97	0.2305	

MEXICO	10 PESOS	8.33	0.2411	1870 TO 1905
	20 PESOS	16.67	0.4823	CALCULATE
	50 PESOS	41.67	1.2057	1.692g/0.0476oz
				PER PESO
SOUTH	1 RAND	3.99	0.1177	
AFRICA	2 RAND	7.99	0.2354	
	KRUGERRAND	33.93	1.0000	
SWITZ-	10 FRANCS	3.23	0.0933	100FR: 1925
ERLAND	20 FRANCS	6.45	0.1867	(BUT NOT 1934 &
				1939) IS IN
				PROPORTION
UNITED	1 SOVEREIGN	7.99	0.2354	$\frac{1}{2}$, $\frac{1}{4}$ AND $1/10$
KINGDOM	$\frac{1}{2}$ SOVEREIGN	3.99	0.1177	BRITANNIA ARE
	1 BRITANNIA	33.93	1.0000	IN PROPORTION
UNITED	1 DOLLAR	1.67	0.0484	THESE FIGURES
STATES	2$\frac{1}{2}$ DOLLARS	4.18	0.1208	DO NOT APPLY
	5 DOLLARS	8.36	0.2419	TO COINS
	10 DOLLARS	16.72	0.4838	OF THE
	20 DOLLARS	33.44	0.9675	1840'S

Silver Coins

AUSTRIA

18th & 19th CENTURY	.	DECIMAL FROM 1925
	.	(Schillings)
Kreuzers 350 to 500	.	
$\frac{1}{2}$ & 1 Thaler	.	5S 835 to 1936
- 36mm 900	.	10S 640 to 1973
	.	25S 800
	.	50S 900 to 1973
	.	- then 640
	.	100S 640
	.	500S 640 to 1982
	.	- then 925

AUSTRALIA

925 to 1945	.	50 cent 1966, 800
500 to 1963	.	10 Dollar 1982, 925

BELGIUM

```
900           .           900 or 680 or 835
              .
20c  1850's   .      Franc 900 to 1850 835 to 1918
¼Fr  all      .       2 Fr. 900 to 1865 835 to 1912
½Fr  all      .      20 Fr. 680 1933-5  835 1949-55
50c  to 1914  .      50 Fr. 680 1935    835 from 1939
2½Fr all      .     100 Fr.            835 all
5 Fr to 1868  .     250 Fr.            835 all
```

SUMMARY: 900 then mostly 835

CANADA

5, 10, 25, 50 cents: 925 to 1919 then 800
Dollar: 36mm dia. only 800 (but not 1972 which is 500)
        The smaller 32mm diameter are not silver
$5,$10   925 (1976 Montreal Olympics)

SUMMARY: 925 or 800

FRANCE

Small coins to/incl. 2Fr: Pre-1864 900 then 835
Crown-size coins (5Fr. 10Fr. 50Fr.) all 900

EXCEPTIONS: The smaller 5Fr.(1960-9) is 835
             10Fr. and 20Fr. 1929-39 are 680

LAST SILVER COINS:

```
½Fr. 1Fr. 2Fr.  1920 (835)
5Fr.            1969 (835)
10Fr.           1973 (900)
20Fr.           1939 (680)
50Fr.           1980 (900)
```

SUMMARY; Last century + crown-size coins mostly 900,
others, mostly 835

GERMANY

```
20 Pf      900 to 1876
50 Pf      900 to 1902
½Mk        900   all
1Mk        900   all except 1924-25 which are 500

1 R'Mk     500   1920's
2 R'Mk     500   1920's and 1931
-          625   1930's
5 R'Mk     500   to 1932
-          900   after 1932
```

SUMMARY From 1870s: 20Pf to 1Mk 900; 1R'Mk to 5R'Mk mostly 500

WEST GERMANY

```
 5 Mk to 1974 (currency)          625
 5 Mk to date (commemorative)     625
10 Mk all (1972 Olympics)         625
```

HOLLAND

5 cent, 10 cent, 25 cent, all under 20mm dia.   640

```
Larger coins:   ½ Gulden 945 then 720  1921-30
                1 Gulden 945 then 720  1922-67
                2½ Gulden 945 then 720  1959-66
```

INDIA

```
2 Annas to 1917 (round)  917
¼ Rupee to 1945          917
½ Rupee to 1940          917 then 1941-5  500
1 Rupee to 1939          917 then 1939-45 500
```

SUMMARY; 917 except wartime ½ Rupee and 1 Rupee which are 500

IRELAND

```
Pre-1944            750 (not 3d or 6d)
10/- 1966           835
```

ITALY

```
  20c   835 to 1867
  50c   900 to 1892
Lira    900 to 1943
   2L   835 to 1917
   5L   900 to 1914, 835 to 1941
  10L   835 to 1941
  20L   800 to 1941
 500L   835 (not the two-colour version)
1000L   835
```

SCANDINAVIA

DENMARK AND NORWAY

10 Ore	400 to 1919
25 Ore	600 to 1919
Krone	800 to 1917
2 Kr.	800 to 1917 (Norway)
2 Kr.	800 to 1917 (Denmark)

SWEDEN

10 Ore		400 to 1962
25 Ore	600 to 1919	400 to 1961
50 Ore	600 to 1919	400 to 1962
Krone	800 to 1942	400 to 1968
2 Kr.	800 to 1938	400 to 1968
5 Kr.	800 1962	400 1952-66

Late 1960s to 1980s 10Kr to 200Kr commemorative are 800 to 925

SUMMARY: 3 Standards for circulation coins: 400, 600 and 800;
very small coins (3d-size, 10Ore)   400
small coins (½p-size, 25 Ore)   600
Larger coins (1/- and 2/- size, 1Kr. 2 Kr.) 800

ICELAND   (was part of Norway then Denmark; first coin 1926)

1000 Kr. and 500 Kr. 1974, 925. (there is also a gold 500 Kr.)

SOUTH AFRICA

Look at the portrait: Mr. Kruger   (1892-97)   925
King/Queen   (1923-50)   800
Decimal until 1964   500
1 Rand   800
but from 1979 1 Rand also of non-silver

SWITZERLAND

½Fr. 1 Fr. 2 Fr.	835 to 1967
5Fr.	900 to 1928 then 835 to 1969

UNITED KINGDOM

Pre-1920 925; Pre-1947   500

UNITED STATES

5 Cent	(Nickel)	350	1942-45	(not those with mint mark D)
10 Cent	(Dime)	900	to 1964	
25 Cent	(¼)	900	to 1964	
50 Cent	(½)	900	to 1964,	400 to 1970
Dollar		900	to 1963,	400 to 1970

COMMEMORATIVE MEDALLIONS

Manufacturers of commemorative medallions (private mints) usually sell by mail order, the customer agreeing to buy one medallion per month until a set is complete. Subjects range from famous people, to birds and animals, to buildings and transport, in fact, any subject that attracts the imagination. These medallions are issued in gold, silver, or 'base' metals, often with accompanying presentation folders and books and the designs on them are exquisite. True to the advertisements they are works of art to treasure and keep. Be prepared, however, to pay a high price relative to gold or silver value.

Away from the glossy adverts the market is limited and nearly all medallions end up in the melting pot, artwork and all. If you buy medallions for their beauty you will be well pleased; if you are buying for investment it is probable that you will have to wait a great many years to recover your money. The issue of aesthetic value versus intrinsic value is a personal matter, at least gold and silver always have a value - how many household items thirty years old have any value at all?

In the chart opposite, the first column in the chart shows the number of medallions in the set; the second column gives the metal, as follows:

925	Sterling silver	(925 parts per thousand)
999	Fine silver	(999 parts per thousand)
9ct	9ct gold	(375 parts per thousand)
22ct	22ct gold	(916 parts per thousand)
SG	Silver gilt	(Silver plated with gold)

NAME OF SET OF MEDALLIONS	No.	METAL	Oz.
1000 YEARS OF BRITISH MONARCHY WOODEN, BOX	50	925	105.0
BRITANNIA COMMEMORATIVE SOCIETY,PER BOX OF	6	999	8.0
BRITANNIA COMMEMORATIVE SOCIETY, IN CASE	30	999	40.1
BYGONE DAYS, JOHN BETJEMEN	36	925	38.5
CHAUCER	36	925	38.5
CHURCHILL CENTENARY TRUST	48	925	39.6
CORONATION, VARIOUS KINGS & QUEENS 30mm	1	925	0.5
CORONATION, VARIOUS KINGS & QUEENS 157mm	1	925	3.0
CORONATION, VARIOUS KINGS & QUEENS 15mm	1	925	0.3
DIAMOND JUBILEE, QUEEN VICTORIA 15mm	1	925	0.3
ELIZABETH OUR QUEEN, WOODEN CASE	25	925	20.6
ENGLISH COUNTIES SUNDRY	40	925	52.0
FLAGS OF THE WORLD	138	925	141.7
GENIUS OF JOHANNES VERMEER, WOODEN CASE	31	SG	31.5
GREAT BRITISH REGIMENTS	52	925	75.5
GREAT MILITARY COMMANDERS, PER BOX OF 5	5	SG	141.7
INTERNATIONAL BANKS INGOT COLLECTION	50	925	65.9
KINGS AND QUEENS OF ENGLAND	43	22ct	4.3
KINGS AND QUEENS OF ENGLAND	43	925	55.3
LOUVRE	50	925	65.9
MICHELANGELO, WOODEN CHEST	60	925	77.6
MILESTONES OF MANNED FLIGHT	25	925	25.5
MOUNTBATTEN AND THE SEA, ALBUM	100	925	120.6
PETER SCOTT SERIES	35	925	75.5
PRINCE OF WALES INVESTITURE	1	925	3.6
QUEENS OF THE BRITISH ISLES		925	
REMBRANDT	50	925	106.0
ROYAL PALACES	12	925	12.1
ROYAL SHAKESPEARE CO. THE SHAKESPEARE MEDALS	38	925	49.2
ROYAL WEDDING 1973 FDC	1	925	0.8
SOUTHERN AFRICA WILDLIFE SOCIETY	24	925	28.9
THE 100 GREATEST MASTERPIECES	100	925	212.0
THE QUEEN'S SILVER JUBILEE	4	SG	3.3
THE QUEEN'S SILVER JUBILEE, OVAL	2	925	2.8
THE ROYAL ARMS, SHIELD-SHAPED	EACH:	925	1.5
THE ROYAL SILVER WEDDING	72	SG	
THE ROYAL WEDDING	73		
THE SNOWMAN, CHRISTMAS INGOT	1	925	2.1
U.S. PRESIDENTS	36	925	38.9
VINTAGE CARS, MINIATURE INGOTS	100	925	4
VINTAGE CARS, WOODEN CASE	36	925	75.5
WINDSOR CASTLE, 152mm X 28mm	1	925	3.2
WINSTON CHURCHILL	1	925	2.6

Hallmark Date Letters

HISTORIC HALLMARKS

LONDON FROM 1678-1974

BIRMINGHAM: FROM 1773-1974

1773	1793	1816	1838	1859	1881	1902	1925	1947	1969
1774	1794	1817	1839	1860	1882	1903	1926	1948	1970
1775	1795	1818	1840	1861	1883	1904	1927	1949	1971
1776	1796	1819	1841	1862	1884	1905	1928	1950	1972
1777	1797	1820	1842	1863	1885	1906	1929	1951	1973
1778	1798	1821	1843	1864	1886	1907	1930	1952	1974
1779	1799	1822	1844	1865	1887	1908	1931	1953	
1780	1800	1823	1845	1866	1888	1909	1932	1954	
1781	1801	1824	1846	1867	1889	1910	1933	1955	
1782	1802	1825	1847	1868	1890	1911	1934	1956	
1783	1803	1826	1848	1869	1891	1912	1935	1957	
1784	1804	1827	1849	1870	1892	1913	1936	1958	
1785	1805	1828	1850	1871	1893	1914	1937	1959	
1786	1806	1829	1851	1872	1894	1915	1938	1960	
1787	1807	1830	1852	1873	1895	1916	1939	1961	
1788	1808	1831	1853	1874	1896	1917	1940	1962	
1789	1809	1832	1854	1875	1897	1918	1941	1963	
1790	1810	1833	1855	1876	1898	1919	1942	1964	
1791	1811	1834	1856	1877	1899	1920	1943	1965	
1792	1812	1835	1857	1878	1900	1921	1944	1966	
	1813	1836	1858	1879	1901	1922	1945	1967	
	1814	1837		1880		1923	1946	1968	
	1815					1924			

1705 1706 1707 1708 1709 1710 1711 1712 1713 1714 1715 1716 1717 1718 1719 1720 1721 1722 1723 1724 1725 1726

1727 1728 1729 1730 1731 1732 1733 1734 1735 1736 1737 1738 1739 1740 1741 1742 1743 1744 1745 1746 1747 1748 1749

1750 1751 1752 1753 1754 1755 1756 1757 1758 1759 1760 1761 1762 1763 1764 1765 1766 1767 1768 1769 1770 1771

1772 1773 1774 1775 1776 1777 1778 1779 1780 1781 1782 1783 1784 1785 1786 1787 1788 1789 1790 1791 1792

1793 1794 1795 1796 1797 1798 1799 1800 1801 1802 1803 1804 1805 1806 1807 1808 1809 1810 1811 1812 1813 1814 1815

1816 1817 1818 1819 1820 1821 1822 1823 1824 1825 1826 1827 1828 1829 1830 1831 1832 1833 1834 1835 1836 1837

1838 1839 1840 1841 1842 1843 1844 1845 1846 1847 1848 1849 1850 1851 1852 1853 1854 1855 1856 1857 1858 1859

1860 1861 1862 1863 1864 1865 1866 1867 1868 1869 1870 1871 1872 1873 1874 1875 1876 1877 1878 1879 1880 1881 1882

1883 1884 1885 1886 1887 1888 1889 1890 1891 1892 1893 1894 1895 1896 1897 1898 1899 1900 1901 1902 1903 1904

1905 1906 1907 1908 1909 1910 1911 1912 1913 1914 1915 1916 1917 1918 1919 1920 1921 1922 1923 1924 1925 1926 1927

1928 1929 1930 1931 1932 1933 1934 1935 1936 1937 1938 1939 1940 1941 1942 1943 1944 1945 1946 1947 1948 1949 1950

1951 1952 1953 1954 1955 1956 1957 1958 1959 1960 1961 1962 1963 1964 1965 1966 1967 1968 1969 1970 1971 1972 1973-4

SHEFFIELD FROM 1773-1974

Date letters (hallmark symbols) by year:

Year	Year	Year	Year	Year	Year	Year	Year	Year	Year
1773	1793	1816	1838	1860	1882	1904	1925	1948	1971
1774	1794	1817	1839	1861	1883	1905	1926	1949	1972
1775	1795	1818	1840	1862	1884	1906	1927	1950	1973
1776	1796	1819	1841	1863	1885	1907	1928	1951	1974
1777	1797	1820	1842	1864	1886	1908	1929	1952	
1778	1798	1821	1843	1865	1887	1909	1930	1953	
1779	1799	1822	1844	1866	1888	1910	1931	1954	
1780	1800	1823	1845	1867	1889	1911	1932	1955	
1781	1801	1824	1846	1868	1890	1912	1933	1956	
1782	1802	1825	1847	1869	1891	1913	1934	1957	
1783	1803	1826	1848	1870	1892	1914	1935	1958	
1784	1804	1827	1849	1871	1893	1915	1936	1959	
1785	1805	1828	1850	1872	1894	1916	1937	1960	
1786	1806	1829	1851	1873	1895	1917	1938	1961	
1787	1807	1830	1852	1874	1896	1918	1939	1962	
1788	1808	1831	1853	1875	1897	1919	1940	1963	
1789	1809	1832	1854	1876	1898	1920	1941	1964	
1790	1810	1833	1855	1877	1899	1921	1942	1965	
1791	1811	1834	1856	1878	1900	1922	1943	1966	
1792	1812	1835	1857	1879	1901	1923	1944	1967	
	1813	1836	1858	1880	1902	1924	1945	1968	
	1814	1837	1859	1881	1903		1946	1969	
	1815						1947	1970	

150

MATCHING DESIGNS ON CUTLERY

Cutlery comes in several different designs. It's very common to buy odd pieces. Usually you must spend time pealing the layer of silver off (the inside is a horrible hard sticky substance called Shellac) before you can scrap the silver. However, if you know what the designs are, and if you have enough pieces, you can start matching them.

OLD ENGLISH

TRADITIONAL
(with bone handles)

BEAD

ROSEMOUNT

152

RAT TAIL

QUEENS

REGENCY

GRECIAN

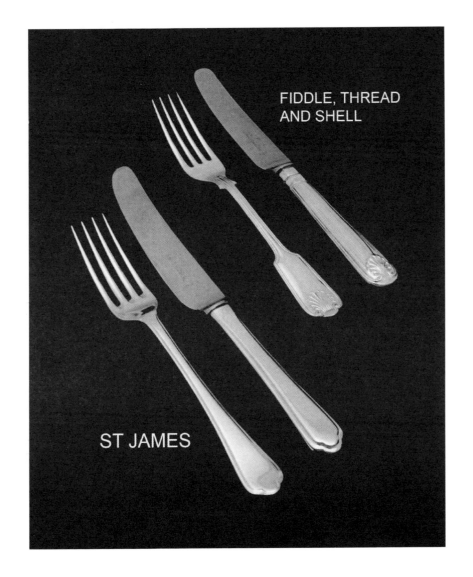

FIDDLE, THREAD
AND SHELL

ST JAMES

ALBANY

FEATHER EDGE

KINGS

DUBARRY

157

JESMOND

GADROON

DESIGNS OF CHAINS

Chains come in many different designs. This applies to any chain (neckchains, bracelets, ankle chains) of any metal (gold or silver). It's useful to know what these are so that you know the choice when buying. It also helps to have a name when selling (items with a name sell more easily).

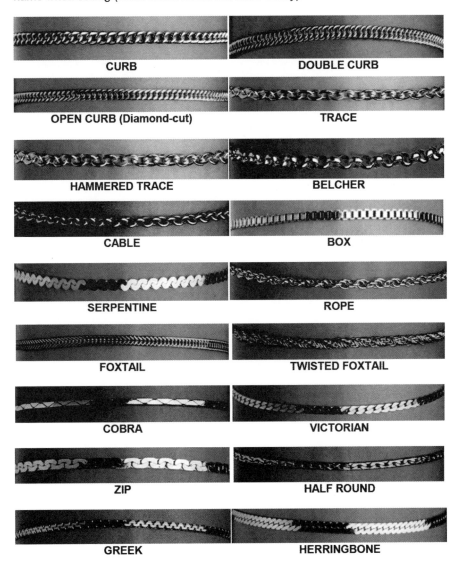

CURB	DOUBLE CURB
OPEN CURB (Diamond-cut)	TRACE
HAMMERED TRACE	BELCHER
CABLE	BOX
SERPENTINE	ROPE
FOXTAIL	TWISTED FOXTAIL
COBRA	VICTORIAN
ZIP	HALF ROUND
GREEK	HERRINGBONE

MORE ABOUT PAPER MONEY AND GOLD MONEY

On page 75 I say that before the First World War paper money was interchangeable with gold. I have found a letter sent to me in 1990, typed on a manual typewriter and unsigned. Here are some extracts:

According to English Practical Banking by Thomas Bouchier Moxon, 1935 (1st edition 1895):

Our currency system is based on the 'Sovereign' which ...weighs 123.274 grains when of standard weight and is legal tender so long as it weighs not less than 122.5 grains. Prior to the restriction of the use of gold, any person who chose to take to the Mint bar gold of the value of £20.00 was entitled to have it returned to him in sovereigns containing the exact amount of gold which he brought, but as the bank of England bought bar gold of standard purity or fineness at £3.17s 9d.per ounce, in practice, all bars were sold to the bank, the loss of 1½d. per ounce being just equivalent to the loss of interest and other expenses...The Bank of England still buys bar gold at its standard price but sovereigns are not returned in payment. The export of gold is now prohibited except under licence....The Coinage Act, 1891, provides that gold coins not more than three grains (whether sovereigns or half sovereigns) below the standard weight may be exchanged by the Mint at their nominal value....Gold coins are a legal tender for any amount, that is to say may be used to discharge any debt.

And (from the same source) upon the subject of banknotes:
Full particulars of the number, date, place of issue and denomination of every note sent by post should be taken, and unless orders are given to the contrary they should be cut in two, and the halves sent by different mails, one letter at least being registered. [The two halves would be stuck back together by the recipient].

Also two copies of letters to The Times, this one dated 18 January 1937:
...How many people have read the inscription, 'I promise to pay the bearer on demand the sum of one pound'?...what is the pound that these notes promise to pay? It may surprise many people to know that there is no such pound...When the Fiduciary issue replaced the Treasury notes under the Act of 1928 many people supposed that the promissory notes referred to golden sovereigns, but those who applied at the Bank for redemption of these notes were met with a refusal. It was then found that only presenting about 1,700 of the one pound notes was it possible to get a bar of gold weighing 400 ounces, and this was the only form of 'redemption' that became legalised. ...As the sovereign to-day is worth over 30s[1]. it follows that the 'promise to pay' can have no reference whatever to gold. Arthur Kitson, Farquhar Road, S.E.19.

...and then on 20 January 1937:
May I suggest that historically a pound is 240 pennyweight of silver? It dates from a time when there was no gold or copper coinage; but there were not only silver pennies but silver farthings. The regular medieval measure of silver was the mark and half-mark; but there were weights, not coins, and the mark consisted of 160, and the half-mark of 80, silver pennies, ie. two-thirds and one third of a pound of silver respectively. We still retain the terminology; 'dwt' is a pennyweight, being a hybrid syncopation of d. for the Latin denarius and 'wt' for weight. The measure of course is Troy weight, in which 20 dwt = one ounce; but it was established as the monetary pound in 1527, was learnt by many of us at school, and was only abolished in 1879. And, while 20 dwt X 12oz no longer makes a pound, 12d X 20s produce the same result; and the half mark or 6s 8d is still familiar as a lawyer's fee for writing a letter. Yours faithfully A.F.POLLARD. Institute of Historical Research.

---

[1] £1.50

CALIBRATING WEIGHING MACHINES

Calibration (in a weighing machine) is the matching of the reading to a unit of weight. If the balance goes out of calibration it will still give higher readings with higher weights[1], but those readings will no longer be 'grams' or 'ounces' and so the balance will be useless. It then needs to be recalibrated.

Every balance will go out of calibration given enough time or if bumped or dropped. In the scientific industry balances have the calibration checked every year. That is why every balance in a laboratory or hospital has a sticky tab with the date it was last checked, a technician will call, and he will charge £75.00 per hour. However, if you have a low-value balance it is cheaper to recalibrate it yourself.

Buy a weight and follow the recalibration instructions in the instruction leaflet. If you don't have any weights, use coins: 5p=3.25g, 1p=3.56g, 10p=6.5g, 2p=7.12g, 20p=5g, 50p=8g, £1=9.5g, £2=12g. For instance, one £2 coin + four £1 coins = 50g. The recalibration instructions can be complicated, you must follow them precisely or you will make it worse. *IF IT IS READING CORRECTLY (OR IF IT IS NEW) LEAVE IT ALONE!*

How often do you have to check the balance? It depends...
Very approximately, if you paid over £400.00, check it every few years; if you paid under £400.00, check it about once a year. Low-value balances are not so reliable: if you paid about £50.00, check it every few months; if you paid about £20.00, check it every few weeks; if you paid about £10.00 there really is no guarantee that it will stay in calibration from one day to the next, this is not a fault, you get what you pay for.

To recalibrate it yourself, you will need a weight (see the instruction manual to find out which weight), this is not included with the balance, you *will* have to find one or buy one (typical price, £5.00 or £10.00).

If you have an approved balance[2] (you will have paid between £400.00 and £800.00) my advice is to leave it alone unless you suspect that the readings are wrong, or unless a Weights & Measures Inspector rejects it. However, you may wish to get it checked once every few years. You cannot recalibrate these yourself, they need to be sent to an approved laboratory and will cost about £100.00.

---

[1] Some balances display an error code instead.

[2] "Approved" means approved for use in trade by the Weights & Measures Authority (part of Trading Standards), if you are buying and selling precious metals by weight, you need to buy one that is approved to a standard called CLASS 2 .

ABOUT TESTING ACIDS:
JUST HOW DANGEROUS ARE THEY?

The main method of testing gold is with acid, and acids are poisonous and corrosive. At one extreme there are users who carry loose bottles of acid in their pocket (a bit like carrying a loose firework in your pocket) and who always manage to splash it on their hands when testing. At the other extreme are users who panic if they get the slightest whiff of fumes or spill the tiniest drop.

Here are four short 'case histories' which will, I hope, put the danger into perspective. You do not have to read this, it is just for the sake of interest.

The Case of the Stained Hand. A lady called to say she had spilt some acid on her hand a few days previously. She said, 'It's stained my hand yellow and I've tried everything to wash it off and my hand is still yellow. What should I use to clean it?' She was horrified to learn that the 'yellow stain' was, in fact, a chemical burn and was not going to 'wash off'. But she was relieved to hear that the skin would grow back over the next few weeks.

CONCLUSION: if you do have an accident with the acid, don't panic, keep calm, wash the acid off under the tap. Many jewellers continually spill tiny drops on their hands and their fingers are always stained yellow. If you are careful there is no reason to *ever* spill drops of acid. If you manage to squirt acid over your skin[1] and *do not* wash it (under a tap for at least three or four minutes) then you are well-advised to seek medical advice.

The Case of the Child. A distraught father telephoned. He had been using the acid and, against all the warnings, had left the cap off, had left it within reach of a three-year-old, and had then left the room. The child spilt the acid down her leg, the parents did not follow the safety precautions, did not wash the acid off, and by the time the child arrived at hospital the acid had burnt down to the bone, the child needed major surgery and will be scarred for life.

CONCLUSION: treat the acid as you would any other household chemical (bleach, ammonia etc): KEEP IT AWAY FROM CHILDREN and if there is an accident, follow the safety precautions.

---

[1] These acids do NOT keep burning through the body as portrayed in some science fiction films. There is an acid that does this (Hydrofluoric acid - it penetrates the skin and dissolves the bones) but it is not used for testing gold.

The Case of the Sudden Illness. A man telephoned to say he had used the acid, had accidentally sniffed some of the fumes, and a few hours later he felt sick and dizzy. He went to his doctor who said that it was most unlikely that his symptoms had anything to do with the acid.

CONCLUSION: regarding sniffing acid: it is not to be advised, and certainly not on a regular basis, it is not good for the lungs. However, don't panic if you accidentally sniff it just very occasionally. There really is no need to rush to the doctor. Jewellers who have various bottles, old and new, will often sort them by deliberately sniffing the fumes, if it makes them cough and splutter it's good - it's a fresh bottle...but this is not to be advised, for instance regular sniffing of blue fluid can cause hydrochloric acid to accumulate in the lungs and over a long period that *will* cause medical problems.

If you don't feel well you might be ill, quite irrespective of the acid, so please do whatever you usually do when you don't feel well.

One word of caution: if you work with other chemicals that also produce fumes, especially if you don't have adequate ventilation, it is possible that the combination of fumes could make you ill.

The Case of the Irritable Eye. A customer telephoned to say that his friend had got some acid in his eye. We asked when this happened and he said a few minutes ago; we asked where the friend was and he said, standing right here. We asked how sore the eye felt and he asked his friend and his friend said quite sore; we gave the official advice which is to hold the eye open under a running tap for at least ten minutes; he asked if he should seek medical advice and (since he had asked) we said yes - we had to assume he had got acid in his eye, we couldn't possibly tell him, 'It's probably nothing', when we had no way of knowing.

CONCLUSION: please be aware of two possible extremes. If the person is screaming with pain as their eye dissolves into their brain, do not telephone us for advice, get that eye forced open under a running tap and dial 999. At the other extreme, if you *think* you may have had some acid on your finger and rubbed your eye but really don't know if you've rubbed acid or dirt (note how black your hands become from dirt when handling old jewellery) - keep calm, the eye 'feeling irritable' does not constitute a major injury, give it a wash and see how you feel in a few minutes. Incidentally, if you wash yourself in icy cold water, the cold will make the skin go completely numb, so do not panic, the feeling will come back when the skin warms.

GEMSTONES and GEM TESTERS

When you buy a gem tester the instructions will tell you how to get readings but not how to interpret them. So if, for instance, you buy a refractometer, you will get a series of readings for each stone, but you must look up standard text books to see what they mean. Here are just a few of the more important 'gem constants' you will need when using a gem tester. Useful as these charts are, they will not turn you into a gemmologist, that takes two years' of study.

KEY RI: Refractive Index (Two readings can be seen when using monochromatic light); DR: Double refraction, the difference between the two RI readings; SG: Specific Gravity (Relative Density).

BERYL   RI 1.57-1.58   DR 0.006   SG 2.71
Emerald   Grass-green
Aquamarine   Sea-green / sea-blue
Beryl   Pink, colourless, blue, violet, yellow

CHRYSOBERYL   RI 1.74-1.75   DR 0.009   SG 3.68 to 3.78
Cymophane   Greenish yellow, cat's-eye effect
Alexandrite   Green in daylight, red under a light bulb

CORUNDUM   RI 1.76-1.77   DR 0.008   SG 4.00
Ruby   Red
Sapphire   blue, yellow, pink, green, purple, colourless

DIAMOND   RI 2.42   DR none   SG 3.51 to 3.53
Preferably colourless but also bluish or yellow

GARNET   RI 1.74 to 1.89   DR none   SG 3.41 to 4.21
Pyrope garnets are red merging into deep red, violet-red and black known as almandine.   Spessartite is brown or orange-red. Grossular garnets vary in colour from a reddish-orange (hessonite) to green ('transvaal jade'). Andradite garnets are found in green (demantoid), yellow (topazolite) and black (melanite).
Uvarovite is bright green.

QUARTZ   RI 1.54-1.44   DR 0.009   SG 2.65 to 2.66
Rock crystal (colourless); amethyst (violet); citrine (yellow); cairngorm (brown); rose quartz (pink); prase (green); tiger's eye (green or   yellow with 'cat's eye' effect); aventurine   (brown, yellow, red or green with specs of mica);   Venus Hairstone (colourless with golden needles of rutile inside)

SPINEL   (Natural)   RI 1.72   DR None   SG 3.60
             (Synthetic)   RI 1.73   DR None   SG 3.64
Red, orange, yellow, pink, blue, green, purple

Gem testing

Often I am asked if there is a simple electronic instrument which will positively identify all gemstones. The answer is no. A few trial models have been launched in the last few years, each sold for upwards of £500.00 and each has been withdrawn due to unreliability. When I speak of 'unreliability' it is not so much the machines that were unreliable as the operators. In the hands of a laboratory technician these testers are quite good - each machine will be kept in one position on a clean bench in a warm draft-free laboratory, used strictly in accordance with the instructions, and checked regularly against known gemstones. Once a jeweller (or, worse, an antiques trader) gets hold of one of these gem testers the story is very different. The machine will be used in workshops or exhibition halls where it is dusty. It will be thrown in and out of brief-cases, left in the car under a scorching sun or used in outdoor markets in sub-zero temperatures and drizzle. And as for checking the calibration against known gemstones regularly - the antiques trader will merely complain that such an expensive machine should work in all conditions and without the need for calibration...forever....and that he's lost the instructions...which he never understood anyway.

Now the good news. A number of long-established and well-tested optical instruments exist which test for all common gemstones. There is also a new generation of very reliable diamond testers. Each of these machines is reviewed below. No one test should be taken as conclusive 'proof' of identity, each test eliminates some possibilities and suggests others.

Natural, Synthetic and Imitation Gemstones

The difference between a synthetic and a natural stone is that one has been grown by nature in the ground over many years while the other has been grown by man in a laboratory in a few weeks. Synthetic gemstones have the same chemical and optical properties as their natural counterparts. This means that - with a few exceptions - synthetic and natural stones give the same readings on gem testing instruments: they *are* the same. Synthetic stones can often be distinguished by the inclusions ('faults') inside the stone which are visible through a good 10X lens or microscope. An *imitation* is when one gemstone appears to be another (of a different chemical composition). Thus, cubic zirconia may *imitate* diamond but it is not - it is cubic zirconia whereas (for instance) a synthetic sapphire *is* a sapphire.

Magnifiers and Microscopes and other Gem Testers

A magnifying lens is by far the most important piece of equipment for the gemmologist. Buy the best you can afford as, in time, it will become your most valuable aid to identification. The standard strength used for gemstones is 10X. Gemmological microscopes magnify between 15X and 30X and have a good working distance. Stronger microscopes are far too strong, you will see only the very surface of a stone and will not be able to focus on the inclusions inside. A good gemmological microscope will include a variable light source and facilities for attaching accessories. A very basic low-power microscope of reasonable quality will cost Between £200.00 and £300.00; a full-fledged gemmological microscope will cost over £1,000.00.

THE REFRACTOMETER (approx. price: a few hundred pounds)

WHAT IT IS: A narrow box with a viewing lens at one end, a slit to let in the light at the other, a calibrated dial on the side and a small flat glass plate on top. A special ('monochromatic') light gives clearer readings than an ordinary table lamp. A refractometer is the most useful piece of equipment after a magnifier or microscope because it gives a reading in figures which is specific to a gemstone or group of gemstones. The reading is known as refractive index, RI.

HOW IT WORKS: Some light in a cut gemstone is refracted (bent) into the stone and some light is reflected out; *some* light grazes the surface of the stone so that it is *just* refracted into the stone - the refractometer measures this 'flip' of light from refraction to reflection, the angle of the 'flip' being unique to each stone.

WHAT IT WILL DETECT: Stones with an *RI* 1.40 to 1.77, that is, most stones.

LIMITATIONS: Only stones with a polished flat surface can be tested, cabochon stones can be tested with difficulty. Zircon and almandine garnet are beyond the range of the machine and so too are diamond and its simulants (Cubic zirconia, YAG, GGG).

HOW TO USE IT: A spot of liquid (supplied) is placed on the glass and the gemstone placed on top. Through the viewfinder one can seen a light area and a dark area. The reading is taken from a scale marked on the dial. Spend several minutes practising, taking readings on known stones, before trying the machine out on unknown stones.

THE CHELSEA FILTER (approx. price: under £30.00)

WHAT IT IS: This looks like a magnifier with a dark lens.

HOW IT WORKS: White light is made up of all the colours of the rainbow (the spectrum: red, yellow, green, blue, violet). Colours are known, technically, as wavelengths of light. A gemstone will absorb some wavelengths and transmit others. It is this 'mingling' of wavelengths that gives the overall illusion of colour. The 'overall illusion' of emerald is that it is a vivid green. Emerald is unique, however, in that it also transmits red, though the eye does not register it. A Chelsea filter filters out all but the deep red and yellow-green so that most emeralds appear red through the filter.

WHAT IT WILL DETECT: The filter was originally designed to distinguish emeralds from imitations, but also helps detect other stones. It will not positively identify any one stone but will separate out different stones: rubies and spinels from paste and most garnets; emerald and beryl from peridot, paste, green sapphire and most tourmaline; cobalt-blue manmade stones (including paste) from natural blue stones.

LIMITATIONS: The Chelsea filter is of little use when examining red stones. As with all gem testers, readings vary according to the chemical make-up of the particular stone you are examining: eg. not *all* emeralds and rubies appear to change colour.

HOW TO USE IT: Hold the filter close to the eye and shine a bright light on the stone. The stone need not be held close to the filter, it can even be in a museum showcase.

THE SPECTROSCOPE (approx. price: under £100.00)

WHAT IT IS: A tube 2" long and ½" in diameter with a lens at one end and a slit at the other. You can see a spectrum through the lens.

HOW IT WORKS: Certain elements ('transitional elements') absorb certain wavelengths (colours) of light. If light from a stone is split into a spectrum the absorbed wavelengths will not be visible. The effect is to see a spectrum in which black or white lines correspond to the 'missing' colours.

WHAT IT WILL DETECT: Ruby, red spinel, many garnets, emerald, sapphire, peridot, pink tourmaline, yellow chrysoberyl, alexandrite, aquamarine, zircon, cobalt-blue glass, cobalt-coloured synthetic spinel, to name but a few.

LIMITATIONS: The stone must have a good colour (with the exception of colourless zircon); readings vary with chemical composition, a perfect 'textbook' reading is rare. It takes practice to both see and recognise the patterns of lines.

HOW TO USE IT: View the colour given off by a gemstone by shining the light from a small pencil torch through the stone (if it is transparent), or by bouncing the light off the stone (if it is opaque) - very fiddly, you may need three hands.

HARDNESS Never use a hardness test on a polished stone. Diamond is the hardest stone known to man and will scratch all other gemstones but non-diamond gemstones can be valuable and should not be scratched. Neither is it wise to scratch a hard stone *with* a diamond: diamond, although hard, is brittle and may chip if maltreated. It is true that a diamond will scratch glass but so too will most gemstones.

HEAVY LIQUIDS By dropping a loose stone into a 'heavy' (dense) liquid its specific gravity (relative density) can be measured by observing if the stone sinks or floats. Ideal for loose parcels of stones but not suitable for mounted jewellery.

POLARISCOPE This comprises an arrangement of polarising filters and a light. It distinguishes singly refractive and doubly refractive stones: diamond, cubic zirconia, garnet, spinel and pastes are singly refractive, most other stones are doubly refractive.

TESTING DIAMONDS, BUYING DIAMONDS

A diamond tester looks like a thick felt pen with a fine metal tip[1], it takes a battery and lights along the side indicate DIAMOND or NOT DIAMOND.

Unlike other gem testers, which are designed for gemmologists, the electronic diamond tester is mass produced for jewellers, antiques dealers, scrap merchants, and aunt Agatha who wants to see if her diamond engagement ring really is diamond. Although cheap diamond testers can be found on the internet for £30.00, a good (reliable) diamond tester will cost between £50.00 and £80.00.

How do you work a diamond tester?

Switch it on, hold it like a pen, wait for it to warm up (when the READY light shows), press the tip onto the stone, if the row of LED lights light up quickly (and there's a bleeping sound) then you have a diamond, if the lights don't move at all it is not diamond, if the lights move very slightly you probably have a ruby or sapphire (though a diamond tester is not designed as a ruby - sapphire tester). There is also a safety feature that sounds an alarm if you accidentally touch the mount instead of the stone (which avoids false readings).

How does it work?

Heat. Or, to be more precise, thermal conductivity. You may have seen traders 'testing' stones to see if they are paste or 'real' by touching the stone against their lip. They are feeling for 'coldness.' Plastics (and maybe glass) feel warm-to-the-touch, many gemstones (probably) feel cold to the touch, it's not very scientific. This relative coldness is what the tester is measuring, thermal conductivity.

Are there different types of diamond tester?

The most common type of diamond tester works on the principle of thermal conductivity. There are two slight variations. The cheaper models have two lights, one for *diamond* and one for *not diamond*, the best model has a row of lights. The advantage of the better model (row of lights) is that you can turn the sensitivity down if you are working in the cold (eg. an early morning market), the cheaper model (two lights) will give false readings if the stone is cold.

---

[1] There are still some very old-style diamond testers about, which comprise a big box of electronics and a probe...but times have moved on.

The diamond tester designed by QUICKTEST has been especially calibrated for Northern Europe where it is likely to be cold, as opposed to the Chinese idea of calibrating them for 'room temperature' only, which is quite warm in China. This is the only diamond tester that will actually give correct results on cold stones[1].

How reliable are diamond testers? - what about cubic zirconia and moissanite?

The two most common diamond simulants are Moissanite and cubic zirconia (including 'diamond-coated' cubic zirconia). The latter presents no problem at all but moissanite needs a special mention. Moissanite is a purely synthetic stone (i.e. it is grown in laboratories by man, it does not exist in nature) and it registers as diamond on diamond testers. This is an unfortunate fact of nature, that moissanite has the same thermal properties as diamond. So how do you tell moissanite from diamond? There is another electronic tester, it looks (and operates) just like a diamond tester though it works on an entirely different principle. Or there is a combined electronic tester for diamond and moissanite.

Do you need a diamond tester and a moissanite tester? Most people buy the diamond tester 'just to start with' and buy a moissanite tester later. Do you really need a moissanite tester? Here are two facts that might help you make your decision:

FACT 1. Moissanite was first commercially grown ('invented') by man in 1995, so if you are quite certain that you are testing an antique ring (that hasn't been tampered with) then the stones won't be moissanite. The origin of moissanite as a mineral (Silicon Carbide) found in meteorites, dates back to 1893, but this cannot be used as gemstones, quite contrary to the publicity that implies that moissanite is a rare as-good-as-diamond gemstone that comes from outer space.

FACT 2. Moissanite hasn't quite taken off in the way that cubic zirconia did, probably because the smallest moissanite costs several pounds whereas cubic zirconia costs a few pennies, so moissanite isn't that common. However, it's main purpose (it seems to me) is to fool antiques dealers, usually with a story about the item of jewellery having been in the family for many years.

So if you are trawling the fairs and boot sales and are happy that the items you see are genuinely old, you will probably be OK with just a

---

[1] A stone might be cold because you are buying at an outdoor market or fair in the winter, or because a customer has brought a stone in from the cold, or because a fraudster has cooled the stone in the knowledge that it will fool diamond testers.

diamond tester, but if you set up shop and advertise that you buy jewellery you will attract the fraudsters, so make sure you have a moissanite tester too.

Finally, there are testers that will test both diamond and moissanite (i.e. one tester to test both). Most models are quite fiddly to use, because the machine first tests for diamond (thermal conductivity) then all the electronics re-set, then it carries out a second test, for moissanite (electrical conductivity), and the electronics get confused and give wrong readings if you move the test-tip by a fraction of a millimetre during the test, or if you don't make firm contact with the stone, or if the stone isn't clean (you must clean it with a cotton wool bud and alcohol).

At the time of going to press, there is only one model we would recommend (the 'Multi' tester for diamond and Moissanite), it is the only model we cannot 'trick' with our selection of 'difficult' stones.

Whichever you choose, you will need good eyesight (good enough to see the tip of the tester and the very centre of the stone clearly) and a steady hand. I have watched many people who have neither of these attributes and will never, ever, be able to use a tester, at best they 'sometimes' get it to work.

ARE DIAMOND TESTERS FOOLPROOF? - THE TALE OF A MAN WHO WAS FOOLED

Nothing is foolproof. Supposing, for instance, you bend the test-tip, fill the tester up with coffee, use a flat battery...

I recommend the type of tester with the row of lights that show how fast the machine is reacting, rather than two pre-set lights that tell you YES or NO. And by far the most reliable (to protect against fraud) is the QUICKTEST model. The following story is a warning to anyone who thinks that having a machine (any machine) is guaranteed to get them a bargain.

We sold a diamond tester to a man who went out to South Africa to buy 'bargain' diamonds (uncut 'rough' diamonds) from a 'contact'. After a very long time haggling they agreed a price (I think it was $50,000.00), he tested the stones, they registered DIAMOND on the tester, they were sealed in a container and he signed across the seals. The money was transferred into the seller's bank account and the following day the buyer collected the stones. The seals on the container were still intact. And guess what? When he got them back to England he had his doubts, rushed the diamonds over to us, we tested them on five different diamond testers - they were not diamonds.

There are precautions you must take if you are spending large amounts of money and know nothing about diamonds.

Most importantly, if the deal seems too good to be true, it's because it is too good to be true, 'Cheap Diamonds' are like 'cheap gold' or 'cheap cash' - they simply don't exist...unless they involve smuggling and other criminal activity, either by criminal gangs who also deal in weapons and drugs, or by armed factions fighting a war. You have been warned!!

Do not let that diamond tester out of your sight, even for a minute. They can be tampered with (by re-soldering wires inside) so that everything reads DIAMOND. Our man in South Africa managed to return to England without the diamond tester. It had been 'mislaid in the confusion' - what a surprise!

Keep on your person a genuine diamond (it need not be large) and a paste (glass) and a sapphire (a small synthetic sapphire will do) and test each of them before testing your purchases. You will then know if the diamond tester has been tampered with. It is also possible, with any machine made by man, that the machine develops a fault - so use those three stones to check the machine.

Tricksters have been know to store stones in ice to cool them so that the diamond tester falsely reads DIAMOND. Try touching the stone gently against your upper lip to see if it feels icy cold, try clasping it in your warm hand and chatting to the sellers for five minutes. If they become agitated it might be because the stone is rapidly reaching room temperature and is about to register NOT DIAMOND on your tester.

All of this advice refers to the type of diamond tester with a row of lights. The type with two lights (they simply indicate YES or NO) are not suitable for buying rough (uncut) stones at all.

None of these precautions apply to everyday dealing where the amounts of money involved are relatively small, there is no need to become paranoid. And I did sell a diamond tester to someone who was going to South Africa, but who had recommendations from friends who lived there, and he was happy about who he was dealing with and, as far as I know, the transaction was successful. Whether he made a profit I have no idea.

DIAMONDS AND U.V. (Ultra Violet light)

Some models of diamond tester have a built-in UV light, and this has led to the quite logical assumption that UV light can be used for testing diamonds. This is not true. There is absolutely no way you can distinguish diamond from non-diamond using UV light. The only useful thing to know is that diamonds fluoresce (glow) randomly. So if you have a cluster ring or a diamond brooch and all the stones react in exactly the same way (whether they fluoresce or not) they are probably not diamond. If some fluoresce and some don't, they might be diamond, they might not.

UV light does, however, have some use for the gemmologist because it can give an indication of probability when comparing natural diamonds with synthetic diamonds.[1]

For examining 'parcels' of diamonds you will need a UV lamp that provides longwave *and* shortwave UV light. View the stones on a black background in a dark room (or UV-viewing cabinet). Natural colourless diamonds, when they fluoresce (about 40% do) usually fluoresce more under long-wave than they do under shortwave, some synthetic diamonds have just the reverse reaction, the fluorescence is weak (or nil) under long-wave, and strong (or stronger) under shortwave. If, therefore, you buy loose diamonds it could be worthwhile checking each parcel under UV light to judge the probable mix of 'naturals' and 'synthetics'. But examining one diamond under UV light will tell you nothing.

UV light can also be useful when grading a diamond for colour. White diamonds that fluoresce under UV light also fluoresce under UV present in daylight, and this can make the stone appear a better colour than it really is, so you may wish to downgrade it by one or two colour grades. All this is for the professional diamond dealer, the average jeweller will not know how to grade diamonds and does not need to know any of this.

MOISSANITE AND U.V. (Ultra Violet light)

Unlike diamond testing, UV light is useful when testing Moissanite (it changes the electrical conductivity and gives more accurate results). If your tester has a built-in UV light, do check carefully that the light stays on *while* you are testing the stones, otherwise it will be completely useless.

---

[1] 'Synthetic' does NOT mean 'imitation' - a synthetic stone is grown in the laboratory to the same recipe found in nature, and the aim of the manufacturer is to make an end-product which is identical to its natural counterpart. Synthetic diamond IS diamond (unlike, for instance, cubic zirconia or moissanite or paste which are not diamond) - and synthetic diamond registers DIAMOND on diamond testers...because it IS diamond.

GOLD / SILVER RATES SURVEY

In the Summer and Autumn of 2010 I sent 'parcels' of gold and silver to several nationally-advertised *We Buy Your Gold!* mail order companies. These gold buying companies mount massive press and television advertising campaigns. They send out prepaid envelopes for your gold, offer quick payment, and their literature is full of examples of the massive amounts they pay out. I sent each of them a mixture of gold and silver, some hallmarked, some not hallmarked.

The rates offered (the percentage of the actual gold / silver value) were low. The worst was £2.45 for scrap with an actual gold / silver value of £32.18, this being 8% of the actual value, the best rate was 23%. Cheques / offers took between two and four working days to arrive, though when I refused an offer it took another week for the goods to be returned. These gold buying companies do have to cover the millions of pounds it costs for press and television advertising, endorsements by celebrities, running call centres and sending out free postage packs, so it is not surprising that they offer low rates.

All through 2010 there was an OFT (Office of Fair Trading) investigation into some of the gold buying companies. The OFT's main complaint was the "business practice of sending consumers a payment, which if not rejected and returned within restrictive time periods, meant that their 'silence' was taken as consent to the payment and their gold was melted down" They concluded that sellers must be given a *choice* between merely accepting a payment, or getting a quotation which they could accept or refuse. Having read this book, *you* understand about gold and scrap and that the value is based on the weight of the gold only, and that the gold will be melted (and any gemstones destroyed) - but none of this is obvious to a lay person, and the OFT now require gold buying companies explain these points.

It's interesting to note that the OFT were *not* investigating the rates offered. If a buyer and a seller agree an amount of money to be exchanged for goods, it's a done deal (in legal terms, a *contract*), the goods are exchanged for payment, and it is too late for either side to complain.

In the Spring of 2011 we searched the internet again, but instead of spending ten minutes and finding the most widely-advertised companies, we spent thirty minutes and found another eleven. I shan't give you any names, because they change from month to month and will soon be out of date, but these companies are not secret, they are all listed on the internet. Of the eleven, three gave no rates, one gave a relatively low rate (62½%) and seven gave very high rates, varying from 94% to 97% of the actual gold value. This time, instead of sending gold to all of them, we chose just one: the company offering 97%. It was genuine, they really did pay us 97% of the actual gold value. But this *was* their 'trade' rate, for which we had to give them our company registration number and VAT number.

Next, I wanted to know how much we would get by taking some gold and silver to the high street.

I found thirteen companies in our local town centre. First I telephoned them. Seven said they were jewellers who didn't buy scrap (one said they would send the gold away for valuation which would take five to six weeks). Of the remaining six, only two gave us a rate per gram, the others said they would have to see the items. I then called on all six with a selection of broken jewellery. Annoyingly, the two that gave a price per gram actually offered far less when I arrived in person. The lowest rate offered was 33% and the highest was 82%. With the price, at the time, just over £10.00 per gram for 9ct, this meant that offers for our gold chain (2g of 9ct) varied from £10.00 to £25.00.

The advantage of selling directly (instead of by mail) is that you can get several offers in a short period of time, make your choice, and be paid cash. When asked (though nobody volunteered the information) all the buyers said that we needed identification, usually photo-ID such as a driving license.

Finally, I took some gold to two antiques fairs. Rates here varied from 88% to 96%. If you visit an early-morning midweek antiques fair, you know that the gold buyers are 'trade', because 'public' do not visit antiques fairs on a working day between 5am and 8am, and the gold buyers will be dealing only with traders. That would explain the relatively high rates offered.

Nobody gets 100% of the actual gold value, if you get 80% you are doing well, 90% is unusually high. However, these high rates are a feature of 'gold fever' sparked by very high gold prices and will not persist when the price of gold falls. This is because of the high *level* of trade that goes with a high gold price.

Dealers can work on narrow margins (three or four percent) when they are turning over tens of thousands of pounds per week, their margins must be higher (maybe ten or fifteen percent) when their turnover is just a few hundred pounds per week. At the time of writing, the price of gold (pure gold) is well over $1000.00 (US Dollars) per ounce (Troy ounce). For details of where to find the latest gold price, see page 45; for details of how to calculate the actual gold value of an item, see page 47.

During the course of my 2011 survey I learnt a huge amount about how high street (and antiques fairs) buyers operate, including how accurate they were at testing, weighing and calculating prices. If you would like to see the full report, visit www.quicktest.co.uk/survey.htm

BIRTHSTONES

Once birthstones related to signs of the zodiac. Over the years the signs of the zodiac have been replaced with months of the year. Colours have been allocated to each month (though they do not always relate to the gemstone) and many of the expensive stones have been replaced with cheaper stones.

MONTH	ORIGINAL STONE	MODERN SUBSTITUTE	COLOUR
JANUARY	GARNET	GARNET	DARK RED
FEBRUARY	AMETHYST	ONYX	PURPLE
MARCH	JASPER	AQUAMARINE OR BLOODSTONE	PALE BLUE
APRIL	SAPPHIRE	DIAMOND OR ROCK CRYSTAL	COLOURLESS
MAY	AGATE	EMERALD OR CHRYSOPRASE	BRIGHT GREEN
JUNE	EMERALD	PEARL OR MOONSTONE	CREAM
JULY	ONYX	RUBY OR CORNELIAN	RED
AUGUST	CORNELIAN	PERIDOT SARDONYX	PALE GREEN
SEPTEMBER	CHRYSOLITE	SAPPHIRE OR LAPIS LAZULI	DEEP BLUE
OCTOBER	MULTICOLOURED	AQUAMARINE OR TOURMALINE	MULTICOLOURED
NOVEMBER	TOPAZ	CITRINE	YELLOW
DECEMBER	RUBY	TURQUOISE OR ZIRCON OR LAPIS LAZULI	SKY BLUE

USEFUL CONTACTS

Publications: Jewellery and Gemstones

These are all organisations and / or publications that I know are good, not a random selection from the internet. However, the summaries (in italics) are copied from their websites.

Emap Limited, www.emap.com

Retail Jeweller Buyer's Guide, www.britishjewelleryyearbook.co.uk/about.asp
The only guide to the UK jewellery sector published in print and online... up to the minute and succinct guide for your industry...Containing contact details on almost 1,500 organisations, providing you with a quick and easy reference to the industry.

Retail Jeweller, www.retail-jeweller.com
The leading watch and jewellery magazine

World Gold Council, www.gold.org

Gold Technology, www.utilisegold.com/resources/
Our jewellery technology magazine, Gold Technology, ceased publication at the end of 2002. As its contents remain valid and useful, we are putting all 36 back issues into the Archive over time. This will serve as useful reference materials for jewellers interested in obtaining a better understanding of jewellery materials and manufacturing technology and Best Practice.

Reed Business Information, www.reedbusinessinformation.com

JCK (Jewelers´ Circular Keystone), www.jckonline.com
The jewellery industry's leading trade publication and industry authority. The only paid publication in the market, it has more than 135 years of experience supplying subscribers the information and innovation they need to run their stores more efficiently.

Gifts & Decorative Accessories, www.giftsanddec.com
A monthly magazine founded in 1917, and with a circulation of 27,000.

Gemmological Association of Great Britain, www.gem-a.com

The Journal of Gemmology - quarterly
A leader in its field, The Journal of Gemmology publishes research papers on all aspects of gemmology, including natural stones and their treatments, synthetics and simulated gemstones. The Journal also carries book reviews and abstracts of articles published in other gemmological publications.

Gems & Jewellery - in conjunction with the society of Jewellery Historians.
Unique in its content, this popular magazine provides a wealth of information on gems and jewellery, from the latest news of gemstones on the market today, to the history of jewellery and manufacturing techniques. Also covered are details of upcoming exhibitions and events, auction news and book reviews. Gems & Jewellery is circulated four times a year to Gem-A members.

The British Jewellers' Association, www.bja.org.uk

The Jeweller, www.thejewellermagazine.com
The Jeweller magazine is the official publication of the National Association of Goldsmiths and is published ten times a year by CUBE. This authoritative publication has a 4,000-strong circulation with a readership of approximately 17,000.

Jewellery in Britain, www.bja.org.uk
You can download a pdf version of Jewellery in Britain from this site

The World Jewellery Confederation, www.cibjo.org

The CIBJO Blue Book
A definitive set of standards for the grading, methodology and nomenclature standards for diamonds, coloured gemstones and pearls, in which the latter incorporates all organic materials. It was initially compiled, and since has been consistently updated, by number of committees, comprised of representatives from trade organizations and laboratories in the diamond, coloured gemstone, cultured pearl and jewellery industries. The standards represented a consensus derived from the broad expertise on the subject within these committees, and also from individuals outside the committees who had expressed an interest in participating in the development of the guidelines. Initially the three publications were printed with different coloured covers-blue for the Gemstone Book, grey for the Diamond Book, and green for the Pearl Book. Today, they are generally referred to as one single entity - the Blue Book.

Raffi's summary of the above: an essential book listing 'correct' names for gemstones.

Publications: The Antiques Trade

Antiques Trade Gazette

Weekly. Annual subscription £79.00
Online services *Price Guide* £5.95 per month, *Auction Alert* £5.95 per month

115 Shaftesbury Avenue, London, WC2H 8AF. 020 7420 6600

This is *the* antiques newspaper for the trade and includes auction previews including international events, editorial on nearly every subject from books to coins to antiques fairs, and also antiques-related news of both trade interest and national interest.

Antique & Collectors Trader

Monthly, £15.00 for an annual subscription
Subscriptions Dept, PO Box 2034, Hockley, SS5 5YW
collectorstrader@yahoo.co.uk

This is given away free at antiques fairs but is also available by subscription. It contains a little editorial and lots of adverts, mostly for antiques fairs and centres.

Collectors Companion

Quarterly. Free.
205 Field End Road, Eastcote, HA5 1QZ
tjgraphics_2000@yahoo.com

This is given away at the antiques fairs but it is also available as a .pdf download from www.thecollectorscompanion.co.uk/images/TCC60_mag.pdf Contains hundreds of adverts for fairs and shops, quite a good fairs calendar, and a smaller auction calendar.

The Car Boot and Fairs Calendar

Two-monthly. £14.00 for a year's subscription
or download it from www.carbootcalendar.com/index.php
or £8.99 annual subscription for online access to 2000 listings.

The Car Boot & Market Calendar
PO Box 1014, Bromley, BR1 9NT, telephone 020 8249 0238

This used to contain mostly listings for boot sales but has grown to include antiques fairs, flea markets, steam rallies and county shows, and auctions Also some good editorial from Fiona Shoop and Bill Tricky.

Books

The *Dealer Guide, English Silver Hallmarks* enables the dating of British hallmarked items from 1544 onwards, £5.00.

International Hallmarks on Silver collected by Tardy. Over 500 pages of marks from around the world. There's also an ingenious index at the back which is in picture order, enabling identification when you don't know which country to look up. £20.00.

Gem Identification Made Easy, by Antoinette Matlins. Explains all the basics of gemmology (optical and chemical properties etc) in an enticing way. Each chapter covers a different gem tester, explaining the theory behind it, its practical uses and limitations, and how this links in with all the other testers. £22.50.

All three books are available from www.quicktest.co.uk

Coins and Notes

THE BANK OF ENGLAND, telephone 0207-601 4444, www.bankofengland.co.uk
They will exchange their own banknotes, however old, providing they are genuine and otherwise in order.

THE ROYAL MINT, telephone 0845 60 88 3000, www.royalmint.com
Modern commemorative coins are issued by The Royal Mint and coins are distributed through coin shops and main Post Offices.

Hallmarking / Assay Offices

British Hallmarking Council. Everything about hallmarking can be found at www.britishhallmarkingcouncil.gov.uk including downloads of their latest booklets.

Assay Offices. The Assay Office is the only authority permitted to hallmark precious metals. They also provide other services such as testing and analysis (including Nickel Content Analysis). Hallmark charts are available from the Birmingham Assay Office.

LONDON	Goldsmiths' Hall, Foster Lane, London EC2V 6BN Tel: 020 7606 7010, the.clerk@thegoldsmiths.co.uk
BIRMINGHAM POB	151, Newhall Street, Birmingham, B3 1SB, 0121 236 6951 Hallmarking: info@theassayoffice.co.uk Gemmological Services: gem@theassayoffice.co.uk Precious Metal Analysis: testing@theassayoffice.co.uk
DUBLIN	Dublin Assay Office, Dublin Castle, Dublin 2, Ireland +353 1 4751286 / 4780323, assayirl@iol.ie
SHEFFIELD	Guardians' Hall, Beulah Road, Sheffield, S6 2AN 0114 231 2121, info@assayoffice.co.uk
ASSAY OFFICE OF SCOTLAND	Goldsmiths Hall, 24 Broughton St, Edinburgh EH1 3RH Tel: 0131 556 1144, admin@assay-office.co.uk

Official Bodies

BIS is the government department for *Business, Innovation and Skills*, www.bis.gov.uk
From here, a useful link is *Business Link* for advice on starting or running a business (or go directly to www.businesslink.gov.uk). Within this department, though not linked from the main website, is **NMO** (National Measurement Office), www.nmo.bis.gov.uk for every detail of every regulation concerning weights and measures including hallmarking, enforcement and contacts: click on *Legislation and Guidance* at the top, then select from the options on the left, *Weights & Measures* or *Hallmarking*. If you are more interested the science of weights and measurements, you will find the **NPL** (National Physical Laboratory) fascinating, see www.npl.co.uk and click on *Science and Technology.*

HMRC (HM Revenue & Customs), www.hmrc.gov.uk/index.htm
for VAT and duties, imports and exports, income tax and benefits

TRADING STANDARDS Institute, www.tradingstandards.gov.uk
A useful link is: *Business Guidance > Fair Trading > Goods and Services*
There is also a section about selling on the internet. If, at any point, you enter your postcode, you will be taken to the Trading Standards web page at your local council.

OFFICE OF FAIR TRADING, www.oft.gov.uk is well known for carrying out investigations into unfair practices. This is a good place to find the latest news but it does not deal with members of the public or traders. If you have a complaint, try **CONSUMER DIRECT**, www.consumerdirect.gov.uk, 0845 040506.

Trade Associations & Professional Bodies

BRITISH JEWELLERY, GIFTWARE AND FINISHING FEDERATION
www.bjgf.org.uk, telephone 0121 236 2657.
Represents many trade associations including The Giftware Association, The British Jewellers Association, Surface Engineering Association, British Travelgoods and Accessories Association, and the Jewellery Distributors Association.

WORLD GOLD COUNCIL, www.gold.org, telephone 0854 040506
Swiss-based non-profit organisation to promote gold.

CUTLERY & ALLIED TRADES RESEARCH ASSOCIATION,
www.catra.org, telephone 0114 276 9736
Product Testing, Technical Consultancy, Production & Test Machine Manufacture, Machine Design, Material Testing, Failure Investigations, Product Design

BRITISH NUMISMATIC TRADE ASSOCIATION
www/bnta.net, telephone 0197 229988
Represents over sixty companies including specialist auctions and bullion dealers.

INSTITUTE OF PROFESSIONAL GOLDSMITHS

www.ipgold.org.uk, telephone 0203 004 9806
Fellows must have a minimum of four years' training followed by at least ten years' full-time employment in casting, chasing & repousse, design, diamond mounting, diamond setting, enamelling, engine turning, engraving, goldsmithing, lapidary, polishing, silversmithing or wax modelling.

NATIONAL ASSOCIATION OF GOLDSMITHS
www.jewellers-online.org, telephone 0207 613 4445
Has a good 'search' facility for finding jewellers, valuers and courses. They also boast, *Trading Standards, industry and the media turn to the Association for advice* [and they have a] *very close association with the International Jewellery Confederation (CIBJO)*

GEMMOLOGICAL ASSOCIATION OF GREAT BRITAIN
www.gem-a.info/education.aspx, telephone 020 7404 3334
There are four internationally recognised qualifications (awarded after an examination): The Foundation Certificate in Gemmology, The Diploma in Gemmology, The Diamond Practical Certificate and The Gem Diamond Diploma. You can study for these exams in thirty countries, but you must have the Foundation Certificate in Gemmology before you can advance to the Diploma in Gemmology exam.

PSP FOR CREDIT CARDS

To take credit cards online you need a **Payment Service Provider** (see page 123):

- HSBC Bank: www.hsbc.co.uk
- ePDQ: www.barclaycard.co.uk/business
- Moneybookers Ltd: www.moneybookers.com/app
- PayPal: www.paypal.co.uk
- PPPay.com: www.pppay.com
- Sage Pay: www.sagepay.com
- Nochex: www.nochex.com
- Allopass: www.allopass.com
- BT Buynet: www.epayments.bt.com
- WorldPay : www.rbsworldpay.com
- Perpetual Payments: www.secure.perpetualpayments.com
- DataCash: www.datacash.com
- NetPayments: www.netpayments.co.uk
- Total Web Solutions: www.payments.totalwebsolutions.com
- NetBanx: www.netbanx.com
- Gate2Shop: www.g2s.com
- SecureTrading: www.securetrading.com
- Safecharge: www.safecharge.com
- PayPoint.net Complete Solutions: www.paypoint.net
- eKashu: www.ekashu.com
- ChronoPay: www.chronopay.com
- WirecardAG: www.wirecard.com
- Bucks.Net Services Ltd: www.bucks.net
- Secure Hosting Ltd: www.securehosting.com

CONVERSIONS

1 ozT (Troy oz) =   0.911 oz   Avoirdupois oz
                          31.1035 g   grams
                          20 dwt   pennyweight
                          480 gr   grains

1 dwt (pennyweight) = 1.555g.

1 Kg (Kilogram)   = 32.151 Troy oz

1lb (Pound)   = 14.576 Troy oz = 453.37g

For details of systems of weights see page 53

TRADERS' EQUIPMENT

Troytest kit tests gold from 8ct to 24ct, and silver. Also distinguishes white gold from platinum and Palladium.

Standard QUICKTEST tester for gold from 9ct to 24ct, and silver. Includes a steel file and a magnet.

Typical jewellers loupes (each folds into a metal casing), the one on the left is illuminated and gives a choice of ordinary white light or UV light.

Typical eyeglasses. The one on the left has an adjustable light, the one on the right clips to spectacles.

Typical *non*-approved weighing machines
(these tend to cost from £10.00 to £50.00)

Typical weighing machines approved for use in trade for weighing precious metals
(£450.00 to £1000.00)

Diamond tester

'Multi'
diamond and
Moissanite
tester

BIBLIOGRAPHY

B.W. Anderson, *Gem Testing* (Butterworths, London, 1971)

Colin R. Bruce, *Standard Catalog of World Coins* (Krause Publications, Iola USA 1984)

Michael A Crawford, *Weighing Coins* (Cape Horn Trading Co, London)

J.T. Graham, *Scales and Balances* and also *Weights and Measures* (Shire Publications Ltd, Aylesbury)

Charles J Jackson, *English Goldsmiths and their Marks* (Dover, London, 1921)

Michael A Marsh, *The Gold Sovereign* (Cambridge Coins, Cambridge, 1980) Cambridge, England

Jim Newmark, *Trade Tokens* (Shire Publications Ltd. Aylesbury)

Peter G. Read, *Beginner's Guide to Gemmology* (Butterworths, London, 1984)

Robert Webtser, *Gems* (Butterworths, London, 1975)

Bradbury's Book of Hallmarks (J.W. Northend Ltd, London, 1991)

Coins of England and the United Kingdom (Seaby, London)